MEDIEVAL PHILOSOPHY
AN INTRODUCTION

F. C. COPLESTON

DOVER PUBLICATIONS, INC.
Mineola, New York

Bibliographical Note

This Dover edition, first published in 2001, is an unabridged republication of a standard edition of the work originally published by Methuen & Co., Ltd., London, in 1952.

Library of Congress Cataloging-in-Publication Data

Copleston, Frederick Charles.
    Medieval philosophy : an introduction / F.C. Copleston.
        p. cm.
    Originally published: London : Methuen, 1952, in series: Home study books.
    Includes bibliographical references (p.) and index.
    ISBN 0-486-42008-6 (pbk.)
        1. Philosophy, Medieval. I. Title.

B721 .C57 2001
189—dc21

                                                      2001028590

Manufactured in the United States of America
Dover Publications, Inc., 31 East 2nd Street, Mineola, N.Y. 11501

CONTENTS

PREFACE

THE impression used to be given by historians of
philosophy that one could profitably jump from
Plato and Aristotle straight to Francis Bacon and
Descartes, omitting all consideration both of post-
Aristotelian Greek philosophy and of medieval
thought. This attitude can, of course, be explained;
but it cannot be defended with adequate reasons;
nor would there now be any strong wish to defend it.
For we realize better today the continuity between
medieval, Renaissance, and modern philosophy.
Bacon and Descartes, for example, may have in-
veighed against scholastic Aristotelianism; but
students of Bacon and Descartes are well aware of
the influence exercised upon their thought by the
very philosophy which they criticized. Philosophers
continued for many years to use much the same
categories of thought which had been used by the
medieval philosophers, and to employ in their
philosophy the same principles as the medievals had
employed. It would be a mistake to attribute what
one may call the 'scholastic' elements in philosophies
like those of Descartes, Malebranche or Leibniz to
the influx of, and interest shown in, classical literature in the Renaissance period. Descartes's first
philosophical studies were in the scholastic tradition;
and even if his mind afterwards moved in other
directions the influence of those early studies was
permanent. Indeed, though he sometimes attacked
Aristotelianism for various reasons, he affirmed at
other times that the mental training given in the

1

college where he was educated was a good deal better than that given in many other institutions of a different type. Malebranche was deeply influenced by St. Augustine; and if one asks oneself whether the God of Malebranche bears more resemblance to the God of Augustine, Aquinas, and Scotus, than to the God of Aristotle's *Metaphysics* there can only be one answer. As for Leibniz, he had an extensive knowledge of the philosophic literature of scholasticism, and its influence upon him is apparent in his works. Again, we can trace a connexion between the medieval philosophy of law and that of John Locke, while the latter's empiricism was not so entirely alien to medieval thought as one might be inclined to think. And even Hume's criticism of the concepts of causality and substance was anticipated, in part at least, in the fourteenth century.

But medieval philosophy deserves attention and study not only for historical reasons, because it forms an integral part of the history of European philosophy, but also for its own sake. Although the approach and the setting may be different in different periods, the same, or at least similar, philosophical problems inevitably tend to recur. And even though philosophy is not equivalent to the accumulation of particular facts or items of knowledge which increase in number as the years go on, one is not entitled to assume in advance that the medieval discussions of philosophical problems are worthless, simply because they took place so many centuries ago. Some philosophers would, indeed, say that the methods and aims of the thirteenth-century metaphysicians were mistaken. But that, whether true or false, is a philosophic assertion which is itself open to question and discussion. In any case, an unprejudiced mind should avoid the two extremes of thinking that nothing worth saying or doing has been said or done in philosophy since the Middle Ages and of ruling out medieval philosophy without more ado as intellectual obscurantism. The great thinkers of the Middle Ages were, after all, men of outstanding ability in their time; and it is at least possible that they said something which was worth saying. Claims are sometimes made in a rather naïve manner that this or that modern movement or current of thought has at last set philosophy on a proper basis and given it the right orientation. If one has studied the history of philosophy one realizes that this sort of thing has not infrequently been said before, and one is inclined to read such claims with a mild and amused scepticism or with impatience, according to one's temperament. It would be absurd, of course, to adopt the diehard view that philosophy can be simply identified with the system of some medieval philosopher; but it would be equally absurd to suppose that it can be identified with any system which now lays claim to finality. The comment might be made that no living philosopher does claim that his system, if he has a system, is the final truth; but neither did any reputable medieval philosopher claim that he had said the last word on philosophy. And if one is prepared, as one ought to be, to approach modern systems and ways of thought with a readiness to understand and appreciate, one should approach the systems of the past with a like open-mindedness. If one believes that philosophy can attain truth at all, one can hardly suppose that several centuries of intense philosophic thought produced nothing that was worth the effort expended.

It can hardly be denied, however, that the study of medieval philosophy does present great difficulties to many minds today. Indeed, to many people today medieval philosophy is likely to appear, at first sight at least, as something entirely alien to their conception of philosophy. One of the reasons for this is the close connexion which obtained in the Middle Ages between philosophy and theology. Most of the medieval philosophers were also theologians; and this is true even of William of Ockham. In fact, Ockham cannot be properly understood unless this fact is borne in mind. And this connexion between philosophy and theology undoubtedly influenced the light and the way in which philosophical problems were discussed. Students who do not believe in Christianity are therefore likely to be perplexed by several aspects of medieval philosophy. They are also likely to have much more sympathy with fourteenth-century thought than with that of the early Middle Ages or with that of the thirteenth century. This is quite understandable, since certain late-medieval thinkers approached more or less closely ways of philosophizing to which we have become accustomed today. But it is important to bear in mind that even these thinkers shared the common conviction of the medievals that divine revelation is a source of certain knowledge. Again, one should bear in mind the fact that philosophy does not pursue an isolated path of its own. It is one cultural activity, and it is influenced inevitably by other activities and branches of study which cannot be identified with philosophy itself. We are all aware that the history of modern philosophy cannot be written without taking into account the rise and development of the various sciences. The influence of science on modern philosophy has been profound and far-reaching, even though its influence has not always been uniform in character. In the Middle Ages the principal extra-philosophical factor which influenced philosophy was the Christian religion. Whether one is a believing Christian or not, it is obvious that Christianity is as much an historical datum as modern science; and if one wishes to understand medieval philosophy one must bear in mind the intellectual background of the medieval mind. It is not that medieval philosophy and medieval theology are synonymous terms: it is rather as M. Gilson has shown in his Gifford Lectures, that the Jewish-Christian tradition acted as a powerful fertilizing and stimulating influence in regard to early Christian and medieval philosophy.

A second great difficulty in the way of understanding medieval philosophy comes from the unfamiliar terminology and language. In the first place a knowledge of the Aristotelian philosophy is extremely desirable if one is to understand the meaning of many terms used by medievals and the nature of a large number of problems which they raised and discussed. One must, for example, be able to see when the word 'matter' is being used in the sense of Aristotle's 'first matter' and when it is not. In the second place one cannot take it for granted that a word is being used by a medieval writer in the sense which would naturally suggest itself to an English reader. For instance, the Latin word *species* may be used in one context to mean species, in the sense in which we talk about species and genera; but in another context it may mean a mental modification or idea. Again, 'good' may have the meaning which it has when we say of an action that it is a morally good action; but it may also be used by a medieval philosopher as what was called a transcendental term denoting being in relation to a will or appetite. In this book I have tried as far as possible to simplify terminology and to avoid presupposing a knowledge of the Aristotelian philosophy. But any student who wished to acquire a more extensive and profound knowledge of medieval philosophy would have to make a study of the language of that philosophy. By 'language' in this connexion I do not mean the Latin language, but rather the terminology and categories of thought.

In view of the present direction of philosophic thought in this country it may be appropriate to say a word on the medieval philosopher's attitude towards what is now called linguistic analysis or the clarification of language. One cannot find, of course, in medieval philosophy an analysis of meaning and a treatment of language of the extensive and yet detailed type which would be considered desirable today; but it would be a great mistake to think that the medieval philosophers were blind to the necessity of any linguistic analysis. The problem of the meaning of terms and statements naturally presented itself to their minds primarily in relation to the terms predicated of God and the statements made about God in the Bible. For example, if it is said that God is 'wise' or 'immutable', in what sense are these terms being used? The medieval philosophers saw clearly enough that in a case like this there is a

PREFACE 7

of analogical predication and of analogical language.
The question they asked, however, was what is the
meaning of such terms and statements rather than
whether they have meaning: that they must have
some meaning would have seemed clear to them from
the fact that such terms were used in the Scriptures
and documents of the Church and that they belonged to a realm of discourse with which they were
familiar from youth. But some of the leading medieval philosophers were very much alive to problems
of language. Indeed, a valuable and interesting
monograph could be written on the philosophy of
language, explicit and implicit, of the medieval
philosophers.

Finally, it may be as well to point out that the
phrase 'medieval philosophy' no more means any
one particular philosophical system than does the
phrase 'modern philosophy': it means simply the
philosophizing of the Middle Ages. In point of fact
there was a great deal of variety in medieval philosophy. There is, for example, a profound difference
between the philosophy of Aquinas in the thirteenth
and the philosophy of a Nicholas of Autrecourt in
the fourteenth century. I have tried to bring out
something of this variety in the present work.

CHAPTER I

ORIGINS AND CHARACTER OF
MEDIEVAL PHILOSOPHY

1. PERHAPS the year of Charlemagne's coronation as emperor, A.D. 800, might be taken as a fitting date for the beginning of the medieval period of philosophy. But medieval philosophy had its roots in the ancient world; and it is necessary to know something of early Christian thought, in order to understand the philosophy of the Middle Ages. When the emperor Justinian closed the philosophical schools of Athens in 529 and the non-Christian Neo-platonists left for Persia, a century had elapsed since the death in Africa of St. Augustine while the Vandals were besieging his episcopal city of Hippo and the Roman Empire was faced with final ruin. But, though Augustine's life was passed in the last days of the Western Roman Empire, his writings exercised a profound influence on the thought of the medieval world that was at length to rise out of the Dark Ages. The early medieval philosophers had not a great deal of material at their disposal; but what they had was a legacy of the ancient world.

The Apostles and their successors were primarily concerned, of course, to preach the Christian religion, not to elaborate philosophical systems. But even in the early days of Christianity it was naturally felt to be necessary to defend the new religion against attacks made on it by non-Christian thinkers, to justify its existence in the eyes of the imperial authorities, and to show that true wisdom was to be found in Christianity rather than in the writings of the pagan philosophers. Thus there arose works like the *Apology* of Marcianus Aristides (*c.* A.D. 140), addressed to the emperor Antoninus Pius, the *Plea for the Christians* of Athenagoras (*c.* A.D. 177), addressed to the emperors Marcus Aurelius and Commodus, and the writings of St. Justin Martyr (*c.* A.D. 100–164). One certainly could not call the writings of the early Christian apologists philosophical works; nor could one apply this name to the writings against the Gnostics; but use was made, none the less, of terms and ideas taken from Greek philosophy. Moreover, the early Christian writers were forced to adopt some definite attitude towards Greek philosophy. This attitude varied from the hostility and contempt of a Tertullian to the much more favourable attitude which generally predominated, especially in regard to Platonism. And when the Fathers of the Church started to develop Christian theology, attempting to understand, as far as they could, the Christian doctrines which they accepted by faith and to systematize these doctrines, they made use of ideas and categories of thought which were already at hand, especially in Platonism. The term 'Platonism', however, must here be understood in a wide sense, as denoting the Platonic tradition. Platonism was commonly regarded by Christian thinkers as having been an intellectual preparation for Christianity; but Plato was interpreted in the light of Neo-platonism.

The use of philosophical terms and concepts in the statement of a doctrine like that of the Trinity remains within the sphere of theology. In the early

Christian period, however, there was no clear-cut distinction between philosophy and theology. The position was rather as follows. The writers of the patristic age attempted to understand, state clearly, and systematize to a certain extent the Christian religion: their attitude can be summed up in the famous Latin phrase, *Credo ut intelligam*, 'I believe in order to understand.' They also attempted to interpret the world, man himself, and human history in the light of the Christian faith. They thus occupied themselves (to an extent varying with individuals) with themes which, in terms of the later distinction between theology and philosophy, would be called philosophical themes. St. Augustine, for example, considered subjects like the relation of soul to body in man and the nature of human knowledge; and what he had to say on these matters exercised a considerable influence on medieval thought. I shall say something presently about Augustine's philosophy; but first of all I wish to develop a little further the subject of the relation of philosophy to theology, since an understanding of the problem involved is essential to an understanding of medieval philosophy. If one wishes to understand the philosophy of a given epoch, one has to make the attempt to understand the mentality and presuppositions of the men who lived in that epoch, irrespective of whether one shares that mentality and those presuppositions or not.

The cardinal fact to remember about the early Christian thinkers and about the philosophers of medieval Christendom is that they believed in a definite divine revelation. This revelation, enshrined in the Scriptures and in tradition, was for them a premiss, something given, which they accepted on faith. The attempt to state these doctrines in terms of a clear-cut language, largely borrowed from philosophy, and to develop their implications by logical reasoning led in the end to the growth of scholastic theology. On the other hand, it is obviously possible to start at the other end, so to speak; to start, that is, not with premisses which are regarded as revealed data, but with the objects of human experience, man himself and the world in which he finds himself. Reflection on these immediate objects of human knowledge, and on the knowing process itself, leads to the development of philosophy. In the thirteenth century, St. Thomas Aquinas found the difference between dogmatic theology and metaphysical philosophy to consist primarily in a difference of method. There are some truths which are peculiar to theology, like the mystery of the Trinity, which the philosopher cannot know by means of the unaided natural reason; and there are other subjects, such as the constitution of natural bodies, which do not fall within the sphere of dogmatic theology. But the distinction between theology and philosophy cannot be primarily a distinction of subject-matter, for there is a certain overlapping: the distinction between the two sciences (the medievals spoke of both theology and philosophy as 'sciences', employing the word in the sense of a discipline which gives certain knowledge) is primarily one of method. To take a concrete instance. For the theologian the existence of God is a premiss, while for the metaphysical philosopher the existence of God is known as the conclusion of a process of reasoning based on reflections on the experienced world.

The two methods were employed, in point of fact, from the beginning; but the formal distinction between theology and philosophy was not clearly drawn until the concrete development of philosophical themes forced the distinction on men's attention. St. Augustine in the ancient world and St. Anselm in the early Middle Ages were certainly aware of the difference between what they believed on authority, by faith, and what was the result of their own process of reasoning; but they made no very clear distinction between the two sciences. They were more concerned with what one might call a total Christian wisdom, with understanding the Christian faith itself and with understanding the world in the light of that faith, but without marking off clearly the sphere and the range of philosophy from those of theology. One of the main factors which brought about the drawing of a clear and methodical distinction between the sciences was the introduction of the main body of Aristotelianism to the knowledge of Christian thinkers in the second half of the twelfth and the early part of the thirteenth century. For acquaintance with a grand-scale philosophical system which obviously owed nothing to the Christian religion drew their attention sharply to the need of delimiting the two sciences in a methodical manner. It has sometimes been supposed, especially, of course, by those who did not know very much about medieval philosophy, that Aristotle acted as a curse and a blight, or at least as an intolerable burden, on medieval thought. But this is very far from having been the case. It was largely through the introduction of Aristotelianism to the Christian West that philosophy became, as it were, self-conscious and mature.[1] It was not that Aristotle supplanted and drove out Plato. For, although the early medievals had been influenced by the thought of Augustine and the Pseudo-Dionysius, who had themselves been influenced by the Platonic (or Neo-platonic) tradition, they knew little of the writings of Plato. Indeed, at no time did the medievals possess any extensive knowledge of Plato's dialogues. If, in the thirteenth century, Aristotle came to be regarded as 'The Philosopher', this was due in part to the fact that Aristotelianism was the one philosophical system of which the medievals possessed a wide knowledge. Not all were enthusiastic in their reception of Aristotelianism, as we shall see; but the contrast drawn tended to be between Aristotle on the one hand and St. Augustine and the Christian writers on the other. Conservatives like St. Bonaventure may have praised Plato at the expense of Aristotle; but this was because of remarks made by St. Augustine and the use made of certain Platonic theories by Augustine, and not because of any particular knowledge of Plato's philosophy as such.

The adoption of Aristotelianism by a man like Thomas Aquinas in the thirteenth century involved, of course, the critical re-thinking of the philosophy of Aristotle in such a way that an imposing synthesis of theology and philosophy resulted. The thirteenth century was, indeed, remarkable for the production of such syntheses. Metaphysics, particularly what is generally known as 'natural theology', formed, as it

[1] This is an historical judgement. To emphasize the historical importance of Aristotelianism in medieval thought is not necessarily to state that the Aristotelian philosophy is undiluted truth. The point should be obvious; but misunderstandings can arise, as experience shows.

were, the junction-point of the two sciences. In the following century, however, the criticism which was directed by William of Ockham and those associated with the Ockhamist or 'nominalist' movement against the metaphysical arguments of their predecessors tended to the separation of philosophy from theology, not only through a theoretical recognition of the difference of method between the two sciences, but also in the sense that philosophy was judged incompetent to give that support to theology which it had previously been thought able to give.

One possible way (though not, of course, the only way) of distinguishing the various stages of medieval philosophy is to distinguish them by reference to the relation of philosophy to theology. In the early Middle Ages the distinction between theology and philosophy had not been clearly worked out, partly owing to the rudimentary character of philosophical development at the time. In the thirteenth century the distinction was clearly recognized; but the leading figures in the intellectual world of the period were, for the most part, primarily theologians; and they constructed great syntheses of theology and philosophy, in which the two sciences were harmonized. In the fourteenth century this synthesis tended to fall apart.

To give an outline of the course of medieval philosophy from this point of view is probably to over-emphasize one particular aspect. But it is, none the less, an important aspect. In different historical epochs there exists what one may loosely call a common mentality or mental background, the influence of which can be observed in the literature and philosophy of that period. In the modern era, for example, the immense advance of the empirical sciences has helped to produce a mentality and outlook which is reflected in various ways in philosophy. In the Middle Ages the mental outlook which was reflected in philosophy was largely formed by the common acceptance of the Christian faith. Thus, medieval philosophers were often profoundly interested in problems which would not appeal to a philosopher whose mental background was opposed to theirs. This is not to say that the most important problems studied by the medieval philosophers are not precisely those problems which constantly recur in the history of philosophy. The important problems concerning knowledge, psychology, the moral law, the existence of God, human society, which were discussed by philosophers in the Middle Ages are analogous to problems which have commonly been topics of philosophical discussion ever since. But the language employed, that is to say, the philosophic idiom employed, was rather different from that commonly used today; and the approach to problems was often different. One is constantly made aware of the influence of the theological background, even in the case of a thinker like William of Ockham.

The presence of this theological background should not make one underestimate either the seriousness with which the medievals pursued their philosophic studies and discussions or the high level of philosophic thinking which they attained. Their philosophic language and terms are not fashionable in Britain today; but the care with which they used their terms compares very favourably, to put it mildly, with the respect for language shown by some well-known philosophers of a much later date. As a further point, it is worth pointing out that the accusation of 'wishful thinking' which has been brought against medieval (and not only medieval) metaphysicians can be grossly overdone. For example, it is fashionable to say that when a medieval philosopher set out to prove God's existence, he already believed in the conclusion of the argument on other grounds, with the implication that the proof is therefore considered worthless. It is true, of course, that when Aquinas or Scotus discussed proofs of God's existence they did not suspend belief in God; and it is true that the fourteenth-century philosophers who considered the philosophic proofs offered by their predecessors to be no more than probable arguments did not on that account cease to believe in God. From the philosophic point of view, however, the relevant question is whether a given argument, considered on its merits, is valid or not; the fact that a philosopher already believed in the conclusion on other grounds has no bearing relevant to the value or worthlessness of the argument considered in itself. This point ought to be so obvious as not to need mentioning; but the fact that it has been entirely neglected in certain quarters makes it desirable to mention it.

2. After these general remarks I wish to return to early Christian thought and to say something about three philosophers of the ancient world who exercised a considerable influence on medieval philosophy. The first and most important of them is St. Augustine, who was born in 354 and died as bishop of Hippo in 430.

Augustine's mother was a Christian; but in his youth he became for a time an adherent of the dualistic doctrine of the Manicheans, according to which there are two ultimate principles, the one responsible for good, the other for evil. Augustine was a man of strong bodily passions; and the Christian idea that a good God created all things, including matter and the human body, seemed to him absurd. In the course of time, however, the reading of certain Neo-platonic treatises convinced him that evil is not something positive, the creation of which would have to be ascribed to God if God created all things, but rather a privation. Moral evil, for example, is a privation of right order in the human will, while blindness, a physical evil, is a privation of vision. In general, Neo-platonism facilitated Augustine's intellectual conversion to Christianity; and after his subsequent moral conversion, narrated in his *Confessions*, he was baptized at Milan by St. Ambrose in 387. In the course of his life as a Christian priest and bishop he wrote voluminously; and as time went on he became more and more immersed in theological problems. But in the earlier stages of his career as a writer the influence of Neo-platonism is marked.

Augustine had a strong interest in problems connected with knowledge. That the human mind can attain certainty was for him a fact beyond any reasonable doubt. Reflection will convince any man, he said, that he cannot doubt his own existence, and that he cannot be deceived in thinking that he exists. By his famous phrase, 'If I am deceived, I exist', Augustine anticipated Descartes. One cannot, he thought, deny or even doubt one's existence without talking nonsense. But, though Augustine answered the sceptic in this way, he was much more interested in our apprehension of necessary and immutable truths than in his anticipation of Descartes. Take, for example, a mathematical proposition like $7+3 =10$, a proposition which today would generally be called 'analytic'. As Plato before him, Augustine was impressed by the necessity and immutability of such propositions. Truths of this kind rule, he thought, the human mind: they are discovered by the human mind, and they are neither created nor alterable by the human mind.

Two questions then arise. What is the implication of the independence of these truths in regard to the human mind? And how is it that the human mind, which is itself mutable and fallible, can attain certainty in this way? The answer to the first question is, according to Augustine, that necessary and immutable truths depend on the eternal ground and foundation of all truth, namely God. In other words, the existence of eternal truths which are superior to the human mind implies or reveals the existence of the eternal being, God. Augustine gives various arguments for God's existence; but his favourite line of argument was that based on the human mind's apprehension of eternal truths. This line of argument reappears in some modern philosophies, in that of Leibniz, for example. The second question, how we attain certainty of this kind, was answered by saying that the mind, which is mutable and fallible, is enabled to attain absolute certainty by means of a 'divine illumination'. This light, which is natural in the sense that it is given to every man, irrespective of his spiritual and moral condition, enables the mind to apprehend the elements of necessity and immutability in the judgement.

The divine illumination also enables the human mind to make judgements about things in their

relation to the eternal ideas or standards. We speak
of things as being more or less beautiful, of actions as
being more or less just, of men as approximating to
or falling short of the ideal. Augustine, like Plato,
assumed that judgements of this kind imply the
existence of eternal 'ideas' or standards; but Augustine followed the Neo-platonists in 'placing' these
exemplar ideas in the divine mind. They are the
ideas in accordance with which God creates. We do
not perceive the divine ideas directly. Some historians have supposed that this is what Augustine
meant; but he cannot have really meant this. To
perceive the divine ideas directly would be to enjoy
the vision of God; but even atheists can judge of
things according to unchanging standards. Augustine certainly speaks in different ways at different
times, and it is not easy to say exactly what he
meant—probably he had no very clear idea himself;
but it is at least certain that he thought of the divine
illumination as enabling the mind to make judgements involving a reference to eternal standards. In
other words, Augustine's 'divine illumination' per-
formed a function analogous to that of Plato's
'reminiscence'. Augustine may have toyed for a
time with the notion of the soul's pre-existence, but
in any case he came to reject it. Consequently he
could not say that the soul 'remembers' what it saw
in a state of pre-existence. Instead, he postulated
the activity of a divine illumination.

The two doctrines of the divine ideas and of divine
illumination passed over to the Middle Ages. The
statement of the former doctrine was refined, by
thinkers like Aquinas, in order to purify it of anthro-
pomorphism; but it was an integral part of scholastic

metaphysics. In the fourteenth century William of Ockham rejected it, for reasons which will become apparent later. The theory of divine illumination, however, was characteristic of the so-called Augustinian tradition, which was commonly represented by the Franciscan philosophers, though Duns Scotus discarded the theory on the ground that it was neither a necessary nor an effective help in explaining human knowledge.

It has been the custom to group together a number of theories as characteristic of 'Augustinianism'. Among these is the theory of divine illumination. Another theory is that of the germinal forms or principles (*rationes seminales*). In order to reconcile the statement in Ecclesiasticus xviii, 1 that God created 'all things together' with the account of successive creation in Genesis, Augustine supposed that the species which did not appear at the beginning of the world were originally created in germinal forms which were later actualized. The name he gave to these germinal forms or principles was a translation of the Greek phrase, *logoi spermatikoi*, taken over by the Neo-platonists from the Stoics. It is clear that in asserting the existence of such forms Augustine was concerned with an exegetic problem in connexion with the Scriptures, and not with any evolutionary theory in the modern sense. It is, then, an anachronism to read transformistic evolution into Augustine.

But Augustinianism was also partly a matter of spirit or direction of interest. The theory of divine illumination, for example, emphasized God's activity within the soul and the dependence of the human mind on God. Again, Augustine was much more interested in the mind's discovery of God through reflection on its own nature and activity than in working out any proof of God's existence of the type found in the *Metaphysics* of Aristotle. There is a certain atmosphere of 'interiority' in Augustinianism, which can be contrasted to some extent with the more impersonal attitude of the medieval philosophers who were strongly influenced by Aristotelianism. This atmosphere pervades the thought of St. Bonaventure in the thirteenth century.

Another writer of the ancient world who is of some importance for medieval philosophy is the Pseudo-Dionysius, who was probably a Christian monk and composed his treatises at the end of the fifth century. As he passed himself off as St. Paul's Athenian convert, his writings came to enjoy great esteem and authority. However, as they reflect the teaching of Proclus, the Neo-platonist, it became clear in the course of time (though not in the Middle Ages) that they could not have been written by Dionysius the Areopagite, but must have been composed at a much later date.

The Pseudo-Dionysius attempted, not altogether successfully, to reconcile the Neo-platonic theory of the One with the Christian doctrine of the Trinity, and the Neo-platonic idea of emanation with the Christian doctrine of creation. This attempt to synthesize Christianity and Neo-platonism influenced very strongly the system of the Irish philosopher, John Scotus Eriugena, in the ninth century. But two points should be mentioned on which the Pseudo-Dionysius exercised a more far-reaching influence. The first of these is his theory concerning our philosophical knowledge of God, or concerning the way in which we speak about God. He distinguished two ways of approaching God by philosophic reasoning, the negative way and the affirmative way. The way of negation consists in denying of God the names or terms we apply to creatures. For example, the creature is mutable: God is not mutable. This method of speaking rests on a recognition of the inadequacy of human concepts when applied to the infinite; and it emphasizes the divine transcendence. The affirmative way consists in predicating of God those attributes of creatures which are compatible with infinite spiritual being. For example, God is called 'wise'. This way rests on the recognition of creation and of the finite reflection of God in creatures. The Pseudo-Dionysius (who did not invent these ways) liked to combine them by speaking of God as 'super-wisdom' and so on. The use of the two ways was common among medieval philosophers. They discussed analogical predication and the problem of the justification and meaning of the terms predicated of God. The second of the two important points to which I alluded is the Pseudo-Dionysius's theory of evil as a privation. I have already mentioned this theory in connexion with St. Augustine; but, as worked out by the Pseudo-Dionysius, it was taken over and utilized by the medieval philosophers. It reappears in modern philosophy in the system of a thinker like Berkeley.

St. Augustine, then, and still more the Pseudo-Dionysius, bequeathed to the Middle Ages philosophies impregnated with elements taken from Neoplatonism. At the same time, however, a certain amount of Aristotelianism was transmitted to the early medievals by writers like Boethius, the author of the celebrated work *On the Consolation of Philosophy*. Boethius, who lived from about 480 to 524, translated into Latin and commented on the logical works of Aristotle, as well as Porphyry's *Isagoge*. He originally intended to carry out a plan, never completed, of translating and commenting on all the works of Aristotle; but we do not know exactly how far he proceeded in the execution of this plan. In any case his translation of the logical works, as well as his own original treatises, furnished the early medievals with a knowledge of the Aristotelian logic. In his treatises mention is also made of several Aristotelian metaphysical doctrines; but it is clear that in the early Middle Ages Aristotle was regarded principally as a dialectician or logician. In addition, the medievals received through the treatises of writers like Cassiodorus and Martianus Capella the idea of the seven liberal arts; grammar, dialectic, and rhetoric (the so-called *Trivium*), arithmetic, geometry, music, and astronomy (the so-called *Quadrivium*).

In spite, then, of the Dark Ages which separated the fall of the Roman Empire from the Middle Ages, the medievals did not have to start again entirely from the beginning. On the other hand, there was a great quantity of the philosophical literature of the ancient world which was either lost or was not available to the early medieval scholars and thinkers. When philosophy began a fresh period of development, its beginnings were modest and restricted in scope.

CHAPTER II

EARLY MIDDLE AGES (1): THE PROBLEM OF UNIVERSALS

1. IN 455 the Vandals took and pillaged Rome, which had already been entered by the Visigoths under Alaric in 408. In 476 the nominal Roman emperor, resident at Ravenna, was deposed by Odoacer, who had risen to a position of eminence among the German mercenaries in Italy; and envoys were sent to Zeno, the Byzantine emperor, to say that there was no longer any Western emperor. Odoacer, with the title of patrician, was effective ruler of Italy, until in 493 Theodoric, king of the Ostrogoths, made himself ruler of the land. It was during his reign that Boethius was put to death, on the charge of having carried on a treasonable correspondence with Byzantium. The Ostrogoth kingdom in Italy lasted until Belisarius, the great general of the emperor, Justinian, took Rome in 536 and Ravenna in 540. But in the second half of the century the Lombards invaded Italy. The rule of the Lombard monarchs was, however, confined to Northern Italy, while the representatives of the Byzantine emperor resided at Ravenna. Rome itself passed under the temporal sovereignty of the pope.

It is understandable that philosophy scarcely flourished during the turbulent years of the fall of the Roman Empire and the successive invasions. Even though the Goths were by no means entirely barbaric, what learning existed was to be found chiefly in the monasteries. St. Benedict lived from 480 until 543; and the monasteries which owed their inspiration to his Rule became the channel whereby some of the old Latin culture was transmitted to the 'barbarian' peoples. (At the same time that one pays a debt of grateful recognition to the Benedictine foundations one must not forget the cultural influence of the old Celtic monasticism, which spread from Ireland to Scotland and northern Britain.) The monasteries remained the centres of culture up to the time of the rise of the medieval cities; and when Charlemagne inaugurated his revival of letters he relied very largely on the co-operation of monks and monastic institutions.

The renaissance of letters came in the time of Charlemagne. In 406 Clovis, king of the Franks, was converted to Catholicism; and under his rule and that of his successors all the Frankish states were united under the Merovingian dynasty. After the death of Dagobert I, however, in 638, the Merovingian kings were only nominal rulers, the real power being exercised by the Mayors of the Palace. Thus Charles Martel, who in 732 defeated the Saracens at Poitiers and halted the Mohammedan invasion in the West (as it had already been halted in the East beneath the walls of Byzantium by Leo the Isaurian in 718), was not king of the Franks in name, but only in fact. In 751, however, the Merovingian dynasty was finally extinguished, when Pippin the Short was acclaimed king of the Franks, with the pope's approval. He left the kingdom to his two sons, Charles and Carloman. The latter died in 771, and Charles, who was to be known as Charles the Great or Charlemagne, became sole Frankish king. After an invasion of Lombardy, several conquests of the Saxons, the annexation of Bavaria, the subjection of Bohemia and the conquest of parts of Spain, Charlemagne was the greatest Christian monarch in Western Europe; and on Christmas day in the year 800 he was crowned emperor by the pope in Rome. This act marked the break between Rome and Byzantium, while it also emphasized the Christian reponsibilities of the ruler and the theocratic character of the Christian State.

But Charlemagne was not only a conqueror. He was also a reformer, interested in educational work and aiming at the cultural reconstruction of society. He gathered about him a band of scholars, of whom the most celebrated was Alcuin of York, who was a product of the flourishing culture which had grown up in Anglo-Saxon England. This English scholar organized the school or academy (the Palatine school) attached to the imperial court, and instructed the pupils in the Scriptures, ancient literature, logic, grammar, and astronomy. He also busied himself with the composition of treatises or text-books and with the accurate copying of manuscripts, particularly of the Scriptures. Among his pupils was the famous Rhabanus Maurus, 'preceptor of Germany', who became abbot of Fulda and subsequently archbishop of Mainz.

It cannot be said that much original work was done by Alcuin and his friends; but their great task was the dissemination of existing knowledge and learning. This was done both in monastic schools, like those attached to the monasteries of St. Gall and Fulda, and in the episcopal or capitular schools.

These schools existed primarily, though not exclusively, for those who were to become monks or priests; but the Palatine school, which some people like to regard as the remote ancestor of the university of Paris, in spite of the fact that Charlemagne's court was at Aachen, was doubtless intended by the emperor to be an instrument in the creation of what we might call a civil service. The language employed in education was Latin; for the use of Latin was necessary for administrative purposes owing to the medley of peoples comprising the empire, even if its use had not followed naturally from the ecclesiastical character of education. It must also be mentioned that one of the principal effects of Charlemagne's educational work was the multiplication of manuscripts and the enrichment of libraries.

Politically speaking, the Carolingian empire was a failure, in the sense that it lost its unity on the great emperor's death. But it was in the ensuing years of internal strife that the first eminent philosopher of the Middle Ages, John Scotus Eriugena, lived and worked. Born in Ireland, John Scotus crossed to France and was attached to the court of Charles the Bald before 850. This monarch was king of the western part of the empire, Neustria, from 843 until 875, when he was crowned emperor. He died in 877, and John Scotus appears to have died about the same time.

In addition to a rather unhappy incursion into the theology of predestination John Scotus translated from Greek into Latin the works of the Pseudo-Dionysius, which had been presented to Louis the Pious (also called 'the Fair') in 827 by the then Byzantine emperor. At that period a knowledge of

Greek was more or less peculiar to the Irish monasteries; or, if found elsewhere in the West, was due to
the influence of Irish monks. John Scotus had studied
in an Irish monastery, though he was probably a
layman. But it is not so much for his translations
and commentaries that John Scotus is remarkable
as for his work *On the Division of Nature*, consisting
of five parts and composed in dialogue form. Even
taking into account his knowledge of and dependence
on the writings of the Pseudo-Dionysius and of
Greek Fathers like St. Gregory of Nyssa, John
Scotus's work was a remarkable achievement, for it
contained a complete system. One receives the impression of a powerful and outstanding mind, limited,
of course, by the conditions of the intellectual life
of the time and by the paucity of the available
philosophic material but none the less rising far
above the rather mediocre abilities of its contemporaries.

The word 'Nature' in the title of John Scotus's
work means the whole of reality, including God and
creatures. The author tries to show how God in
Himself, 'Nature which creates and is not created',
generates in the divine Word the eternal divine ideas,
'Nature which is created and creates', which are the
patterns and causes of creatures. Finite creatures
themselves, 'Nature which is created and does not
create', are depicted as the divine manifestation or
theophany; and finally John Scotus speaks of the
return of creatures to God, the conclusion of the
cosmic process, when God will be all in all, 'Nature
which neither creates nor is created.'

The whole system is an interesting combination
of Christian and Neo-platonic themes, without any

clear distinction being drawn between theology and philosophy. Fundamentally it is a sustained attempt to state the Christian faith and a Christian philosophy or interpretation of the world in terms of the categories and ideas which the author borrowed from sources which were themselves deeply coloured by Neo-platonism. This is not to say, however, that it is a patchwork: its different elements are welded together to form a system. At the same time it is undoubtedly true that in the process of expressing Christian doctrines in what he regarded as the proper philosophic form John Scotus made statements which were incompatible with orthodox theology, though such statements are often balanced by statements with a different import, which help the careful reader to interpret the intended meaning of the first set. It seems to me unlikely that the author actually meant to propound an evolutionary pantheism of the type suggested by some of the things he says. The precise significance of the work is matter for dispute; but it would be out of place to discuss John Scotus's system at any length in a short sketch of medieval philosophy, not because it lacks intrinsic interest, but rather because the work was taken very little notice of at the time. It was utilized by a certain number of writers, it is true; but it was not until 1225 that it acquired some notoriety. It had been appealed to by the Albigensians and was used by Amalric of Bene in favour of pantheism, with the consequence that it was condemned in that year by Pope Honorius II.

The achievements of Charlemagne appeared to augur well for the future of cultural and intellectual progress; but after his death the principle of tribal monarchy soon reasserted itself. The empire was divided; and the period of invasions recommenced. The year 845 witnessed the burning of Hamburg and the sack of Paris by the Northmen or Vikings, while in 847 Bordeaux suffered a like fate. The Frankish empire was ultimately split into five kingdoms, frequently engaged in wars with one another. Meanwhile the Saracens were invading Italy; and they nearly captured the entire city of Rome. Western Europe, apart from the flourishing Moslem culture in Spain, was involved in a second Dark Ages. The Church fell a victim to exploitation by the new feudal society. Abbacies and bishoprics were used as rewards for laymen or unworthy prelates; and in the tenth century the papacy itself was under the control of local nobles and factions. In such circumstances the educational reform inaugurated by Charlemagne could bear no fruit.

In 910, however, the great abbey of Cluny was founded; and the Cluniac reform (which was introduced into England by St. Dunstan) exercised an immense influence on monastic and cultural life in Western Europe. In 963 Otto the Great was crowned emperor at Rome; and the empire was, in a sense, revived under a German dynasty. I say 'in a sense', because the German emperors never ruled effectively over the extent of territory which had formed the Frankish empire of Charlemagne. The foundation of the German empire had, however, an important effect on the Church. It was a scandal of Western Christendom that in the tenth century the spirit of the Cluniac reform was not reflected at Rome. But in 1046 Henry III nominated a German bishop to the Holy See; and this intervention meant that the papacy was finally set free from the control of local nobles. In 1059 Pope Nicholas II entrusted the elections of popes to the college of cardinals; and thus the Church asserted her independence of the temporal power, even of the emperor. The terrible years of degradation were over for the papacy.

In the more settled conditions of life which succeeded the gradual dissolution of the Frankish empire with all the attendant miseries of invasions and wars, that is, in the new feudal society of the early Middle Ages, philosophical activity could begin again. It began, as one would expect, in a very modest way, and it was naturally connected with problems suggested by the available literature. One of the chief problems which exercised the minds of the early medievals was the problem of universal terms or class-names; and I now propose to outline the course taken by the discussion of this problem.

2. Take two statements like 'John is a man' and 'Dogs are animals'. In the first statement 'John' is a proper name, referring to a certain individual, while 'man' is a class-name, denoting a species. In the second statement the word 'dogs' denotes the class or species, while 'animal' denotes a wider class, a genus, of which dogs constitute a sub-class. We are constantly using class-names. If I make the general statement that arsenic is poisonous, I do not mean to say simply that one particular bit of arsenic is poisonous; I am making a universal statement, that all members of the class 'arsenic' are poisonous. Now, I know very well what I am referring to when I make a statement about 'John'. Unless I am making a grammatical statement about the word 'John',

I am referring to a definite individual, whether real or, as in a work of fiction, imagined. But what am I referring to when I use a class-name like 'man'? To a collection of individuals, or to an essence or nature? When I say that 'man is mortal', am I saying that all individual men who have lived have, as far as I know, proved mortal, or am I saying that it is of the essence or nature of man as such to be mortal? If the latter, what precisely is this essence or nature? What is its relation to individual men considered as individuals?

Needless to say, I am stating the problem in simple terms; but, in dealing with the early medieval philosophers, it would be out of place to do otherwise. They discussed particularly two sorts of class-names, species and genera; and they asked themselves whether species and genera, like 'man' and 'animal', are mere words, or whether they are words which express simply ideas or concepts, or whether they denote actually existing specific and generic entities. Or one can put the question in this way. Do species and genera possess a merely verbal existence, or do they possess an intramental existence, in concepts, but not an extramental existence, or do they possess an extramental existence? The problem of universals is constantly recurring in the history of philosophy; but in the early Middle Ages it took a simple form, namely that of asking what is the ontological status of species and genera. It took this form largely because Boethius, in his commentaries on the *Isagoge* of Porphyry, quotes Porphyry as raising the question whether genera and species subsist as such, or whether they exist only as concepts, and, if they subsist or exist as such, whether they are in sensible things or separate from them. Boethius's own discussion of the matter was not properly understood; but the question raised originated the controversy in the early Middle Ages. It may be noted that the question as formulated is an ontological question. It is connected with the psychological question, how our universal ideas are formed; but it is not precisely the same question.

The earliest solution given to this problem in the Middle Ages was that of an extreme and somewhat naïve realism.[1] Boethius, explaining the opinion of Aristotle, had said that, according to this opinion, the idea of humanity or human nature is formed by comparing the substantial likenesses of numerically different human beings and considering this likeness separately or in abstraction. The universal idea is formed by thought; but this does not mean that it has no objective foundation outside the mind, even though it has no extramental existence as a universal. The ultra-realists, however, supposed that the order of thought and the order of extramental existence correspond exactly. Thus our idea of 'man', of humanity or human nature, corresponds to and reflects an extramental unitary reality, existing not, as Plato thought, in 'separation' from individual men but in individual men. It follows that there is in all individual men only one substance or nature; and Odo of Tournai (d. 1113) was not afraid to draw the conclusion that when a new human being comes into existence what happens is not that a new substance is produced but only a new property of an

[1] Medieval realism in general was the doctrine that universal concepts or terms have an objective foundation in extramental reality. Extreme realism was the theory that to the universal specific concept in the mind there corresponds an extramentally existing universal specific essence or substance.

already existing substance. This view rests on the supposition that to every name or term there corresponds a positive reality, a supposition which had been apparently maintained by Fredegisius, Alcuin's successor as abbot of St. Martin's at Tours. Ultra-realism was also maintained by Remigius of Auxerre (d. 908), John Scotus Eriugena and, apparently, by St. Anselm (d. 1109). Logically speaking, this form of realism might result in philosophical monism. For, if we had unitary concepts of substance and being, or if we used the words 'substance' and 'being' univocally, all substances should be modifications of one substance and all beings modifications of one being. This is not to say, of course, that the medieval ultra-realists actually drew this conclusion, though the tendency to do so is visible in the system of John Scotus Eriugena.

The ultra-realists, as historians have pointed out, philosophized as logicians. They assumed that the logical and real orders are parallel. One can also say, indeed, that they were misled by language; since they thought that, just as a definite thing corresponds to the name 'John Smith', so a definite thing, an existent universal, corresponds to a word like 'humanity' or 'man'. But it is a mistake to say simply that such people were misled by language, as though that were a sufficient and adequate explanation of their peculiar theory. For example, Odo of Tournai's queer notion that there is but one substance in all men was due partly to theological considerations. Regarding original sin as a positive infection, as it were, of the soul, he did not want to say that every individual human substance owes its existence directly to God, as God would then be

responsible for the positive stain or infection constituting original sin. Instead he said that the one
human substance or nature, infected by sin through
Adam's free act, is handed on at generation. St.
Augustine himself had, for a time, inclined to a form
of 'traducianism', in order to explain the doctrine of
original sin.

The adversaries of ultra-realism maintained as
their guiding principle that only individuals exist;
and this was the principle which was destined to
prevail. Already in the ninth century Eric of Auxerre
had observed that it is impossible to point to any
separate reality exactly corresponding to a word like
'white' or 'whiteness'; if one wants to explain what
the word denotes, one has to refer to a white object,
like a white man or a white flower. For purposes of
economy the mind 'gathers together' individual men,
for example, and forms the specific idea. Similarly,
the idea of the genus is found by 'gathering together'
species. What exists extramentally is simply individuals. An even more trenchant statement of the
anti-realist position was made by Roscelin (d. 1120),
who roundly affirmed that the universal is a mere
word (*flatus vocis*). He was attacked by St. Anselm,
largely because of the application of his 'nominalism'
to the doctrine of the Trinity. But it is difficult to
know exactly what Roscelin's theory of universals
was, as we have to rely mainly on the testimony of
hostile critics. What is certain is that he attacked
ultra-realism and affirmed that only individuals exist
outside the mind. But it is not clear whether his
statement that universals are mere words was simply
an emphatic denial of ultra-realism or whether
he meant to deny the existence of any universal

concepts, supposing that he gave any real consideration to this matter.

The dispute between the ultra-realists and their
opponents came to a head in the famous controversy
between William of Champeaux (d. 1120) and Abelard (1079–1142). The former taught at the Cathedral School of Paris, until the pressure of criticism by
Abelard led to his retirement to the abbey of St.
Victor, whence he subsequently emerged as bishop of
Châlons-sur-Marne. Abelard, the most acute thinker
of his time, lectured in various places during his life;
but his incursions into theology drew upon him the
unremitting hostility of St. Bernard. Accused of
heresy, he was condemned at the Council of Sens in
1141; and he died in retirement at Cluny. Though a
stormy petrel and a man of difficult character and
combative disposition, he was undoubtedly a brilliant
mind and one of the high-lights of the earlier Middle
Ages. At present I am concerned solely with the part
he played in the controversy about universals; some
other aspects of his philosophical activity will be
touched on in the next chapter.

William of Champeaux maintained that one and
the same essential nature is present in every member
of a given species. As the consequence of this would
be that individuals of the same species differ only
accidentally from one another, and not substantially,
Abelard observed that Socrates and Plato must
really be the same substance, and that in this case
Socrates must be in two places at once, if Socrates
is in one town and Plato in another. (As a matter of
fact it would not follow that *Socrates* would be in
two places, for the word 'Socrates' would refer to
the substance with certain accidental modifications

which would be present in only one place. But it would certainly follow that the same substance would be present in two places under different accidental modifications.) Abelard commented that a view of this kind must ultimately lead to monism or pantheism. The subsequent course of the controversy is not altogether clear; but in any case William gave up his doctrine and adopted another. He said that members of the same species are not the same essentially, but 'indifferently'. He most probably meant that two men do not possess identically the same, that is, numerically the same nature but that they possess similar natures or, as he puts it, the same nature 'indifferently'. Abelard treated this theory as a mere verbal subterfuge; but most probably it amounted to an abandonment of ultra-realism. In any case ultra-realism was finally abandoned by William; and the victory rested with Abelard.

The latter went on to say that universality is predicable of words alone; and it might appear, then, that he was a 'nominalist'. But he makes it clear that he is not speaking of the word as a physical entity (*flatus vocis*) but of the word as expressive of a logical content. The universal is not a *vox* or *flatus vocis*, but a *sermo* or *nomen*, a word or name expressing a logical content. What is this logical content? Abelard uses language on occasion which would imply that for him the universal concept is nothing but a confused image, as though, for example, my idea of man is simply a confused image in the mind resulting from the sight of many individual men. Elsewhere, however, he makes it clear that universal concepts are formed by abstraction. If, for instance, I consider

a man as a member of the class of substances,
I am predicating of him the content of a universal
concept which I have formed by abstraction from
actual substances. The universal concept, expressed
by the common word or name, exists, of course, in
the mind; but that which it signifies exists also extramentally, though not as a universal. For example,
it is only individual substances which exist extramentally, and these substances are different kinds
of things; but I can attend to them precisely as substances, and I can thus form the universal concept
which is predicable of each of them. Socrates is not
Plato, whether he is considered as man or as substance; but Socrates is a substance and Plato is a
substance. This is the objective fact which enables
me to predicate the same term of both. But the
sameness belongs to the concept, not to Socrates and
Plato: the two are alike, but they are not the same.
From the linguistic point of view, I predicate a word,
the same word, of each of them; and in this sense it
can be said that universality belongs only to words,
though it belongs to words considered in regard to
their logical meaning, not to words considered as
physical entities or *flatus vocis*. In reply to the question what corresponds in extramental reality to a
universal concept, Abelard would answer that individual things correspond to the concept, that is,
individual things which are alike to one another,
though not numerically the same. In reply to the
question how these concepts are formed Abelard
would answer that they are formed by abstraction.
As already mentioned, Abelard sometimes speaks
ambiguously, implying that universals are confused
images; but substantially his theory is that of

'moderate realism', subsequently adopted by St. Thomas Aquinas.

Although in the twelfth century the members of the school of Chartres inclined to ultra-realism, two well-known figures connected with that school, Gilbert de la Porrée (d. 1154) and John of Salisbury (d. 1180) broke with the older tradition. According to the latter, anyone who looks for genera and species outside sensible objects is wasting his time: genera and species are not things, and they may be said to be mental constructions; but they are formed by abstraction and possess an objective reference and foundation. A similar doctrine was proposed by Hugh of St. Victor (d. 1141), who maintained that, though lines do not exist apart from material things, the mathematician abstracts them and considers them in abstraction. In a similar way the forms of things, their natures, do not exist as universals: but they are considered in abstraction as universals. Finally, in the thirteenth century, St. Thomas, who held that matter is the principle of individuation, maintained that the mind abstracts the essence of man, for example, from individual men and considers it in isolation, as a universal; but universality, though it has an objective foundation in the specific likeness of individual men, belongs as such to the logical order.

The problem was taken up afresh in the later Middle Ages; but it can be left for the time being. It is clear that Abelard dealt ultra-realism its death-blow, by showing the absurd consequences which follow from confusing the logical and the ontological orders or, if preferred, from confusing different logical types. Was the problem a 'linguistic problem'?

In a sense it certainly was, for it arose out of a consideration of the way in which we speak about things. But it was an ontological problem, in the sense that it could be properly discussed only through reference to the facts, to existent things. It was obviously not a purely grammatical problem.

CHAPTER III

EARLY MIDDLE AGES (2): THE GROWTH OF SCHOLASTICISM

1. IT has already been mentioned that Roscelin, the anti-realist, made incursions into theology. For example, he declared, in regard to the doctrine of the Trinity, that we might well speak of three Gods, if usage permitted one to do so, on the ground that the three Persons must be individual realities, if only individuals exist. The dialecticians not infrequently made cavalier attempts to clear up theological mysteries. Not unnaturally, they wanted to apply the instrument of dialectic in the understanding of a concrete subject; and theological doctrines presented one of the obvious fields for the use of their instrument. The building-up of scholastic theology would, of course, have been impossible without the aid of dialectic; and the aim of the more serious dialecticians was that of understanding, not that of 'rationalizing' in the sense of explaining away. But it was principally their incursions into theology which won for the dialecticians the hostility of those who considered that it would be far better to confine oneself to meditation on the Scriptures and the Fathers. Thus, St. Peter Damian (d. 1072) declared that dialectics were a superfluity and the liberal arts useless. The only proper position for dialectic, he thought, is that of being 'the handmaid of theology'; and we are not entitled to suppose that God is bound to the principles of logic. And we have already seen

that St. Bernard took a poor view of Abelard and his
activities.

A more moderate attitude than that of simply con-
demning dialectic was adopted by Lanfranc, who
died as archbishop of Canterbury in 1089. He maintained, very reasonably, that it was the abuse of
dialectic, and not dialectic itself, which merited
censure. And his successor in the see of Canterbury,
St. Anselm (1033–1109), was both a saint and one
of the chief instruments in the development of
scholastic theology and philosophy in the eleventh
century. Primarily he was a theologian; and his attitude can be summed up in the phrase which I have
already quoted, 'I believe in order that I may understand.' He desired to understand, as far as he could,
the data of the Christian religion. 'I desire to understand in some degree Thy truth,' says Anselm,
'which my heart believes and loves. For I do not
seek to understand, in order that I may believe; but
I believe, that I may understand.' Anselm thus
speaks as a believing Christian, and he stresses the
primacy of faith; but he sets out to understand with
his reason the data of faith. In making this attempt
he contributed to the development of both scholastic
theology and philosophy. In regard to the latter his
name is principally associated with his proofs of God's
existence, especially with one of them which is commonly known as 'the ontological argument'. Among
the articles of Christian belief is included, of course,
belief in God; but Anselm, in company with other
medieval thinkers before William of Ockham, thought
that the existence of God can be rationally proved.
And in terms of the later distinction between dogmatic theology and 'natural' or philosophical theology,

proofs of God's existence fall within the sphere of metaphysical philosophy.

Perhaps it might be as well to point out here that it is not only medieval philosophers who have occupied themselves with considering God's existence. We have only to think of Descartes, Leibniz, Locke, Berkeley, Kant, Hegel, Bergson, and Whitehead. Not all these philosophers considered that one can prove God's existence theoretically: Kant did not think that this was possible, though he was by no means indifferent to the question of God's existence and thought that belief in it is assured as a postulate of the practical reason. But my point is that inquiry into the ultimate existent reality or being is an integral part of metaphysical philosophy and has been so from the beginning. It is a mistake to regard this inquiry as proceeding simply from the 'medieval mentality', unless, of course, one is prepared to attribute a 'medieval mentality' to all metaphysicians, in whatever historical period or milieu they may have lived. But to do this is to be guilty of an abuse of language.

In one of his works, the *Monologium*, St. Anselm gives a series of arguments for God's existence. These arguments are based, for the most part, on two suppositions, first that there are degrees of perfection (of goodness, for example) in the universe, and secondly that when a number of things 'participate in' a perfection they must derive this perfection from a being which is that perfection itself. If there are things which are good, there must be an existent absolute goodness, which is at once the standard and source of limited goodness. This line of argument is Platonic in character; but it appears also, in a rather

rudimentary form, in Aristotle; and it reappears in
St. Thomas's fourth way of proving God's existence.
Needless to say, St. Anselm was not so much concerned with proving God's existence to atheists (he
was not speaking to atheists) as with showing that
the empirical world, with its varying degrees of perfection, manifests God's existence. The idea of hierarchy, of ordered grading and of degrees of being and
of perfection, was firmly rooted in the medieval
mind. Some people would like to make out that this
idea, as applied to the cosmos in general, was simply
a reflection of the social and political conditions of
feudal society. No doubt these conditions did have
some influence on the medieval philosophical outlook; but it must be remembered that the hier-
archical principle and the principle of the objective
degrees of perfection was embedded in Neo-platonism
and in the writings of men like the Pseudo-Dionysius. St. Anselm's arguments, whatever we may
think of their validity or lack of it, do not seem to
me necessarily to involve ultra-realism of the early
medieval type; but they are certainly incompatible
with nominalism.

In the same work St. Anselm considers the reason
why certain predicates, and not others, are applied
to God, the Supreme Being. Wisdom, for example, is
predicated of God because God is absolute perfection,
and it is absolutely better to possess the attribute
of wisdom than not to possess it. But to be corporeal
is not absolutely better than not to be corporeal, but
only relatively. It is better to be corporeal than not
to exist at all; but it is not better to be a corporeal
than an incorporeal or spiritual being. Corporeity,
therefore, cannot be predicated of God. Moreover,

one must not be misled by the similarity in form between the statements, 'God is wise' and 'Socrates is wise', to suppose that God participates in an attribute: He *is* wisdom. It is difficult to make the meaning of the word 'participation' very precise but, so far as St. Anselm is concerned, it should not be understood as meaning that creatures embody bits, as it were, of the divine goodness; that would involve pantheism. Anselm does sometimes use ultra-realistic language which would imply that there is a kind of form of goodness which is actually shared in by all good things; but to participate in goodness or in being really means for him to possess being or goodness in dependence on a cause. Sometimes, however, he does carefully explain the language he uses: as when he explains that the phrase 'creation out of nothing' must not be taken to imply that 'nothing' is a kind of material. To say that the world was created 'out of nothing' is simply equivalent to saying that the world was not created out of anything, that is, out of any pre-existent matter. Even the early medievals were not so entirely blind to the necessity of linguistic analysis as has been sometimes supposed.

St. Anselm is best known, of course, for the famous argument in the *Proslogium*, which is generally called the 'ontological argument'. Desiring to find a brief argument which would prove, by itself, all that Christians believe concerning the divine substance, he thought that he had found what he wanted in an argument which showed the existential implication of the idea of absolute perfection. If God is defined as absolute perfection, as 'that than which no greater can be thought', it is not possible, without involving oneself in a contradiction, to deny God's existence. Why not? Because if God, so conceived, existed merely intramentally, that is, in idea, we could conceive a still more perfect being, namely one which exists not merely intramentally, in idea, but also extramentally, in actual reality. In this case, however, it would be possible to conceive a being greater than the being 'than which no greater can be thought'; but to say this is to involve oneself in a contradiction. It follows that we are compelled to think of absolute perfection, that is, of the being 'than which no greater can be thought' as actually existing; and the absolutely perfect being is what we call 'God'. Of course, if a man conceives the divine anthropomorphically, as a number of gods and goddesses, for example, he can certainly deny the objective reality of the divine in this sense; but the point is the uniqueness of the idea of absolute perfection. If 'the fool' in the Psalms really understood what is meant by 'God', he could not deny God's existence 'in his heart', though he could do so with his lips. For, if he really understood what is meant by 'God', he would see that his denial involved him in a contradiction. St. Anselm, then, was not troubled by the contention of the monk Gaunilo, in the latter's apology for 'the fool', that one might just as well say that the most beautiful islands must exist, because we can imagine them. Anselm denied any parity between the two cases. There is no contradiction involved in denying the existence of the most beautiful islands, because the idea of these islands is not the idea of something which *must* exist. But the idea of absolute perfection, of the being 'than which no greater can be conceived',

is the idea of a being which *must* exist or exists
necessarily.

St. Anselm, it may be remembered, had wanted to
find a simple way of proving the truth of all the
statements which believers make about the divine
substance. He thought that in the argument which
I have just outlined he had found this proof. For
if we ask ourselves what is implied in the notion
of a being than which no greater can be thought
we shall discover the attributes of the divine substance; that is to say, attributes like omniscience and
omnipotence.

St. Anselm's 'ontological argument' has had a
chequered history. In the medieval world it was
utilized, in a rather different setting, by St. Bonaventure; but St. Thomas rejected it. The proposition
'God exists' is, he thought, an analytic proposition
'in itself' (*per se nota quoad se*): indeed, it is the only
analytic existential proposition. God is existence
(*esse*); but of no other being can it be said that it is
existence. This does not mean, however, that 'God
exists' is an analytic proposition as far as we are
concerned (*quoad nos*). Of course, if we define God
as existence itself or as the 'necessary being' the
proposition that God exists becomes a tautology; but
St. Thomas's point was that we are entitled to
describe God in this way only as the result of *a posteriori* arguments based on reflection concerning
finite things. That God exists and that He is existence
or being itself becomes known to us only through
reflection on existent finite things, not through
an analysis of the divine essence of which we
have no intuition in this life. 'God exists' is therefore not an analytic proposition as far as we are

concerned;[1] and any argument from the idea of God as supreme perfection to God's existence is ruled out.

In the post-Renaissance world the argument was employed, in different forms, by Descartes and Leibniz. Kant, however, rejected it. We have, in any case, no *a priori* conception of God's possibility, that is, of God's essence, which would enable us to argue to His existence. Further, the argument implies that existence is a perfection, like wisdom, whereas in point of fact, said Kant, it is nothing of the kind. It is an error to speak of existence as though it were a perfection or attribute of a subject. Hegel, however, utilized the argument, though he did so, of course, within the framework of a system which was very different from the philosophy of St. Anselm. Even today a few philosophers accept it in some form or other. That the argument, whether logically valid or invalid, tends to recur in various forms shows, perhaps, that the idea of absolute being tends to impose itself, as it were, on the mind and that it is at any rate a central idea of metaphysics.

2. One must turn from St. Anselm to Abelard, who was important not only in regard to the universals controversy, which was outlined in the last chapter, but also in regard to the general building-up of scholasticism. In his work entitled *Yes and No (Sic et Non)* he gathered together a large number of passages and statements of opinion, principally from

---

[1] Scotus refused to admit the distinction between a proposition which is analytic in itself and a proposition which is analytic 'for us'. An analytic proposition is one the truth of which is evident from an understanding of the terms. That a greater or lesser number of minds do not possess the requisite understanding in a given case does not affect the character of the proposition concerned.

the Fathers of the Church, which apparently con-
tradicted each other, in order that these apparent
contradictions might be discussed and solutions
found to the problems raised. It is important to
realize, however, that he was not engaged in ridicul-
ing the appeal to tradition or the principle of authority. That in some of his writings Abelard tended to
'rationalize' dogmas, notably that of the Trinity, is
undoubtedly a fact; and this fact helped to win for
him the hostility of St. Bernard. But this tendency
to 'rationalize' was not peculiar to Abelard: we find
even St. Anselm talking about proving the doctrine
of the Trinity by 'necessary reasons'. At a time when
the distinction between dogmatic theology and
speculative metaphysics had not been clearly worked
out, those writers who applied dialectic to the eluci-
dation of the truths of faith tended, not unnaturally,
to indulge in what a theologian of a later age would
call 'rationalization'. But this is not to say that they
questioned the principle of authority in matters of
faith. Abelard certainly did not do so. He expressly
declares, in a letter to Heloïse, that he does not wish
to be a philosopher if it means contradicting St.
Paul nor an Aristotle if it means being separated from
Christ: he pins his faith to the rock on which the
Church is founded. In any case the importance of the
Sic et Non consists in its influence on subsequent
scholastic method. Abelard's method of assembling
mutually exclusive statements and opinions was not
altogether new; but it helped to determine the
character of that method which we find employed in,
for example, the Summa Theologica of St. Thomas.
If one looks at that work, one will find that St.
Thomas gives conflicting arguments and authorities

and then explains and defends his own position. And in the public disputations of the Middle Ages it was the custom for the conflict of arguments and authorities to be followed by the judicial summing up of the professor.

Another important work by Abelard was his *Know Thyself* (*Scito Teipsum*). This may be called an ethical work, though not all the topics dealt with would nowadays be customarily recognized as pertaining to moral philosophy. Abelard examines the character of moral action; and he lays great emphasis on intention. Acts, considered in themselves, are indifferent: it is the intention which makes them right or wrong. It is true that there are inclinations or dispositions which are either good or bad in themselves; but a bad inclination or disposition (a 'vice') is not of itself sin. One can fight against it; and this is meritorious. Sin arises when one consents to evil, or, more precisely, when one does not abstain from doing what one ought not to do. (Abelard expressed the matter in this negative way in order to show that sin is not something positive.) But what does consenting to evil mean? It means acting with disregard of the divine will. Sin consists essentially in an interior act of the will implying contempt for the divine will; whereas right action consists essentially in an interior act which implies respect for the divine will. The exterior act adds nothing in either case. If an executioner legitimately hangs a man out of respect for justice and the law, his exterior act is precisely the same as it would be if he were to hang the man from a motive of private revenge and enmity. But in the first case he acts rightly, whereas in the second case he would sin. And it is the intention

which makes the difference. Moreover, the morality
of acts cannot depend on the goodness or badness of
consequences: consequences are not always in our
power to determine. The intention is all-important.

What, then, of those who died without having
known the Gospel or the law of Christ? If they did
not know the law of Christ, they cannot have chosen
consciously to act against it or intended to despise
it. In this case they cannot have sinned. Are they,
therefore, saved? In the *Scito Teipsum*, Abelard
says that their lack of faith is a sufficient reason for
their damnation, though the cause of this lack of
faith is unknown to us. But in his *Christian Theology*
(*Theologia Christiana*) he utilizes the opinion of those
early Christian writers who said that God had enlightened the pagans through their philosophers, as
He had enlightened the Jews through the Law and
the Prophets. Those pagans who followed the truth,
imparted to them through philosophers who recognized God and the natural law and even divined
something of certain Christian mysteries, were saved.

It is clear that Abelard tended to confuse ethical
issues by introducing purely theological considerations. At least, this is what most modern philosophers would say. Moreover, though a right intention is one of the factors in a moral act, it is not the
only factor to be considered. But the salient point
about his ethical discussions is that he drew attention to and helped to formulate moral problems of
interest and importance, and that through his treatment of those problems he emphasized the interior
and psychological aspects of moral action. In other
words, his treatment of these problems formed a stage
in the development of ethics in the Middle Ages.

His views had to be taken into account, whether they were accepted or rejected in the actual form in which he expounded them.

In a book like this it is hardly possible to give any adequate idea of the acuteness of mind, the thoroughness and the concern for language and verbal distinction which distinguished Abelard's treatment of the problems he dealt with, whether in logic, in theology, or in ethics. It is a great mistake to think of him as being simply a critical and destructive mind. Gilson has well said of him that his influence was 'immense' and that he imposed, as it were, an intellectual standard for his successors. Perhaps this is in some ways the most important aspect of his activity, namely that he lifted the whole level of philosophical thought on to a new plane. This has been shown by the modern study of his writings and influence.

3. St. Anselm died near the beginning of the twelfth century (1109), Abelard near the middle (1142). If one regards medieval philosophy as culminating in the great systems of the thirteenth century, the twelfth century can be looked on as a period of preparation and of partial consolidation. It was in 1158 that the university of Bologna received a charter from Frederick I: but France was the chief intellectual centre of the time, and Paris was coming to be the intellectual centre of France. The university of Paris was not formally constituted until early in the thirteenth century; but the schools of Paris, the amalgamation of which later formed the university, were growing in importance, this rise in importance accompanying the rise of the effective power of the French monarchy. But Paris did not

yet overshadow, as it tended to do in the thirteenth century, all other cultural centres. Bologna was celebrated for the study of law, Montpellier for medicine, while the school of Laon was eminent in the field of theology. Moreover, the pre-eminence of France in the intellectual life of Western Europe did not mean that this intellectual life was not markedly international in character. On the contrary, scholars came in large numbers from other countries, from England, from Germany, and from Italy, to the French schools. Some of them returned after a period to their own countries and there taught and wrote, while others remained in France as professors. If we want to form a picture of the intellectual life of the Middle Ages, we have to think away the boundaries and divisions set up in the modern world by differences of language, religion, national tradition, political and economic conditions. It is true that the medieval German emperor did not exercise any effective control over kingdoms like England and France, and that nationalism was beginning to grow; but the peoples of Europe were bound together by common religious ties, by a common cultural tradition and, in the academic sphere, by a common language, Latin. When Paris came in the next century to be the great intellectual centre of Western Europe, this did not mean that French scholars and professors were necessarily the leading figures. Neither St. Thomas Aquinas nor St. Bonaventure, for example, were Frenchmen.

One of the most prominent and interesting schools of the twelfth century was that of Chartres. It had been founded in 990; but its most flourishing period fell in the twelfth century. Some of the philosophers

of Chartres were greatly enamoured of the *Timaeus*
of Plato and represented nature as an organism,
animated by the world-soul. One of them, William
of Conches, even went so far as to identify the world-
soul with the Holy Spirit; but he subsequently re-
tracted this opinion, explaining that he was a
Christian and not a member of the Academy. But
it was among this group of philosophers associated
with Chartres that the hylomorphic theory of Aristotle made its appearance. According to this theory,
material objects are ultimately composed of 'first
matter', a purely indeterminate principle which cannot exist by itself, and 'form', the determining principle, that is, the principle which makes the thing
the kind of thing it is. Bernard of Chartres, accepting this theory, maintained that the forms of things
are copies of the archetypal ideas in the mind of God.
He thus endeavoured to reconcile Plato and Aristotle,
as John of Salisbury observes. The atomic theory of
Democritus was, indeed, defended by William of
Conches; but in general the school inclined to Platonism in a wide sense.

A pleasing feature of the Chartres school was its
respect for the liberal arts. John of Salisbury, who,
though not educated at Chartres, became bishop of
the city in 1176, had a good deal of hard things to
say about people who wrote a barbarous Latin style.
This distinguished Englishman, who had previously
been secretary to St. Thomas à Becket also wrote on
political and legal matters, utilizing the texts of
Roman philosophers and jurists, as also St. Augustine's *City of God* and the *De officiis* of St. Ambrose.
Although he did not refer the power of the prince to
a pact with the people, as Manegold of Lautenbach

had done in the eleventh century, he insisted emphatically that the prince is not above the law but subject to the law. By this he meant in part the natural law, the existence of which had been maintained by the Stoics. As positive law, enacted by the prince, must at least be in accordance with the natural law, the prince who habitually acts in a manner which infringes natural law or natural justice, or who enacts what is incompatible with the natural law, is a tyrant. And a tyrant may be deposed. Indeed, if there is no other way of getting rid of him, he may be put to death, provided, said John, poison is not the means employed. No doubt John of Salisbury also shared the common medieval view that the prince was subject in some way to the customs of the land and to previous enactments; but he approached the matter mainly through a consideration of the maxims of Roman jurists, not concerning himself much with the conditions and customs of medieval feudal society. But in his dislike of capricious and arbitrary rule he was at one with other medieval theologians and philosophers.

Limitation of space does not permit one to do more than mention another flourishing cultural centre of the twelfth century, namely the abbey of St. Victor outside the walls of Paris. But two figures connected with the abbey were of considerable importance for the development of medieval philosophy. One was Hugh of St. Victor (d. 1141), a German, and the other Richard of St. Victor (d. 1173). These two men did much to further the development not only of dogmatic but also of mystical theology. In the former the mind attempts to penetrate the data of revelation with the aid of

human reasoning, while in mysticism, loving experience of God takes the place of reasoning about
God and the divine mysteries. But the human mind
is also capable of a philosophical knowledge of God;
and both Hugh and Richard developed a series of
philosophical arguments for the existence of God.
Hugh laid some emphasis on self-consciousness as the
basis for one line of argument. Self-consciousness
and introspection bear witness to the existence of a
spiritual soul. But the soul is conscious of its contingency, of the fact that it has not always existed.
It must have been brought into existence; and the
cause of its existence must be God. Though this line
of argument is based on what seemed to Hugh to be
experiential facts and on certain truths of reason
and not on any mystical experience, its psychological
colouring is certainly in harmony with its author's
strong interest in mysticism. As to Richard, though
he included in his series of proofs of God's existence
one from the degrees of perfection, a proof reminis-
cent of St. Anselm's procedure, he also elaborated at
some length an argument from the contingent beings
of experience to the existence of a being which exists
of itself or necessarily. This line of proof became
classical in scholastic philosophy.

Hugh of St. Victor is also important as illustrating
the twelfth-century tendency towards the systematization of existing knowledge and of the various
branches of science and learning. In his *Didascalion*
logic with its various divisions is reckoned as a pro-
paedeutic or preparation for science or knowledge of
things. Science itself is either theoretical, practical,
or mechanical. The former comprises theology,
mathematics, and physics. Mathematics, however,

includes not only arithmetic and geometry but also music, as treating of proportion, and astronomy. Practical science comprises ethics, economics, and politics, while mechanics includes a large number of 'illiberal arts' like medicine, commerce, and even cookery. In this classification, Hugh depended partly on the Aristotelian division of science into theoretical science, which has as its end simply knowledge, and practical science, which aims at a result beyond knowledge itself, and partly on encyclopaedic works of miscellaneous information like the *Etymologies* of Isidore of Seville (*c.* 636). In the Middle Ages the belief in the hierarchic character of the cosmos and in order and teleology in nature and in history naturally inclined the mind to systematization; and such systematization naturally appeared to the medievals an easier task than it does today, not only because of the comparative paucity of empirical knowledge, but also because of a common cultural tradition and a common mental outlook, fashioned and informed by definite principles.

This tendency to systematization showed itself later in the great *Summas* of the Middle Ages; but a prototype of these great theologico-philosophical treatises is found in the twelfth century in Peter Lombard's *Four Books of Opinions* (*Sententiarum*). In this predominantly theological text-book, commonly called the *Sentences*, the author gathered together the opinions of the Fathers, especially St. Augustine, on theological doctrines; and these opinions were grouped systematically in four books, dealing respectively with God, creatures, the incarnation and redemption, and the sacraments and four last things. The work does not show much originality or speculative ability on the part of the author; but it none the less exercised a great influence. It was lectured and commented on by many Scholastic theologians and philosophers, including St. Thomas, St. Bonaventure, Duns Scotus, and William of Ockham. Indeed, it formed a kind of text-book of theology up to the end of the sixteenth century. Some of the topics treated of were philosophical in character; and if we want to know the philosophical ideas of Duns Scotus, for example, or of William of Ockham, we have to consult their commentaries on the *Sentences* of Peter Lombard, as well as their other works. The medieval professors were much given to the practice of commenting on texts in their lectures, and, though the works of Aristotle came to provide the text-books for philosophical commentary, lectures on the *Sentences* formed a definite part of the university curriculum in the thirteenth and fourteenth centuries.

CHAPTER IV

ISLAMIC AND JEWISH PHILOSOPHY: TRANSLATIONS

1. DURING the twelfth and the first half of the thirteenth centuries a great quantity of philosophical literature was made available to the philosophers and scholars of Western Christendom. It is not possible to narrate at any length or at all fully the story of the transmission of Greek philosophical works, particularly those of Aristotle, to the Arab world and, finally, from the Arab world to the Christian world of Western Europe; but some idea at least must be given of the course of events.

The channels by which Greek thought passed to the Arab world was the Christian schools of the Orient. Works by Aristotle, Porphyry, and other Greek philosophers, mathematicians, and medical writers were translated into Syriac at the Nestorian school of Edessa in Mesopotamia (closed by the emperor Zeno in 489), at the schools of Nisibis and Gandisapora in Persia, and at Monophysite schools in Syria. This, then, was the first stage, namely the translation of Greek works into Syriac. The second stage was the translation into Arabic of the Syriac versions of Greek works. In 750 the dynasty of the Abbasides came to power; and a warm welcome was extended by the Arab rulers to Syrian scholars. In 832, a regular school of translators was set up at Baghdad. Some Greek works were, indeed, translated from the original into Arabic; but others were

translated from the Syriac versions. A point to be
noticed is that among the works which the Syrian
scholars transmitted to the Arabs as works of Aristotle there were two which were of Neo-platonic
origin. The so-called *Theology of Aristotle* was really
a compilation from the *Enneads* (4–6) of Plotinus,
while the *Book of Causes* (*Liber de causis*, as it was
known to the medievals) was based on Proclus's
Elements of Theology, though for a time it was
wrongly ascribed to Aristotle. The fact that these
two works passed for works of Aristotle was a fact of
some importance; for it meant that Aristotelianism,
for which the leading Islamic philosophers had a
profound respect and esteem, was seen and presented
in a partly false light. Avicenna, for example, was
strongly influenced by the misnamed *Theology of
Aristotle*.

The third stage was the translation into Latin of
the Arabic versions of Greek philosophical literature.
The work of translation began in the twelfth century,
with Sicily as one centre and Spain as another.
Among prominent translators who worked at Toledo
were John of Spain, Gerard of Cremona, Michael
Scot, and Herman the German. But it is a great mistake to think that the Christian scholars were dependent simply on Latin translations (sometimes
with the vernacular as intermediary) of Arabic versions of Syriac versions of Greek works. Translations
directly from the Greek were made not only in the
thirteenth century, by, for example, Robert Grosseteste and William of Moerbeke, but even in the
twelfth century. Indeed, in some cases a translation
though not always a complete translation, from the
Greek preceded the translation of the same work from

the Arabic. In any case, the translation from the Arabic was often followed by a careful translation from the original Greek. The medievals did not possess an accurate knowledge of the relation of Aristotle to Plato and of the Neo-platonists to both; but to say that they were deficient in knowledge of the history of ancient philosophy is not to say that they did not possess reliable versions of a great part of Aristotle's works.

Through the work of the translators the Christian philosophers and scholars came to possess most of the works of Aristotle, some of the Greek commentaries, and some works by Proclus and other ancient writers. As to Plato, the earlier medievals had possessed the *Timaeus*, or some of it, in Chalcidius's translation; and the *Meno* and *Phaedo* were translated into Latin in the twelfth century by Henricus Aristippus in Sicily. But it was not until the time of the Renaissance that an extensive translation of the Platonic dialogues was made.

But it was not only works by Greek writers which were translated into Latin in the twelfth and thirteenth centuries. Translations were also made of works by Islamic and Jewish philosophers; and these works were of considerable importance for the development of philosophy in Western Christendom. Moreover, the Islamic and Jewish philosophies of the Middle Ages are of interest for their own sake. Unfortunately, space does not permit of anything more than a very brief and inadequate account of these philosophies. A brief account is, however, better than no account.

2. The two most celebrated Islamic philosophers of the Middle Ages are Avicenna (Ibn Sina), belonging to the eastern group, and Averroes (Ibn Rusd),

belonging to the western group. Avicenna (980–
1037), who was a Persian by birth, developed a system which was a fusion of Aristotelianism with a
certain amount of Neo-platonism. Metaphysics, as
Aristotle said, is the science of being. But there are
two main divisions or kinds of being. Of these one
is 'possible being'. This phrase may, however, have
either of two meanings. It may mean purely possible
being, in the sense of that which does not yet exist;
or it may mean actually existent being which owes
its existence to an extrinsic cause. In general, then,
'possible being' means being which does not exist in
virtue of its essence, but which depends for its existence on an extrinsic cause. Possible being is contrasted with 'necessary being', namely that which
exists in virtue of its own essence, that is, self-
existent being. The finite things which compose the
world are all possible beings, depending on extrinsic
causes; and the whole series of possible beings requires as its ultimate explanation a necessary being,
which is God, in whom essence and existence are
identical. This distinction between essence and
existence in creatures, together with their identifica-
tion of God, was adopted by William of Auvergne
(d. 1249); and it formed an important feature of the
philosophy of St. Thomas.

By making God the cause of possible beings
Avicenna did not mean to imply that God creates
freely; on the contrary, creation is necessary. Avicenna tried to deduce the successive emanation of ten
Intelligences, each of which brings into being the soul
and body of a distinct cosmic sphere. The tenth and
final intelligence, associated with the sphere of the
moon, is the cause of the forms which, together with

'prime matter' (the purely potential principle in corporeal things), constitute the objects of sense-experience. It has also the further function of illuminating the human mind and enabling it to apprehend essences in a state of abstraction. It is one and the same in all men, a separate intelligence. But this does not mean that there is no personal immortality; for the individual potential intellect of each man, which is illuminated by the separate Intelligence or unitary 'active intellect', survives death as an individual entity. Avicenna, who was a pious Mohammedan, was thus able to retain the idea of reward and punishment in the next life.

Avicenna's theory of Intelligences was based, of course, on Aristotle's theory of the movers of the spheres; and it reappears in Christian medieval philosophy, the Intelligences becoming angels. But Avicenna's Neo-platonic idea of intermediaries in the process of creation was rejected by Christian philosophers, as was also his idea of creation as a necessary process. As to his doctrine of the separate active intellect, which exercises a function of illuminating the human mind, some Christian philosophers identified the active intellect with God and linked the theory with Augustine's theory of illumination, while others, like Aquinas, rejected altogether the idea of a separate active intellect.

Averroes (1126–98) was born at Córdoba, which was a centre of the flourishing Islamic culture in Spain. In 756 Islamic Spain was separated from the caliphate of Baghdad; and in the ninth century the independent dynasty became the caliphate of Córdoba. A culture arose, of which several famous architectural monuments still remain. such as the

Alhambra of Granada, the Giralda of Seville, and the mosque of Córdoba, which became a Christian church. It was towards the end of the period of Islamic culture in Spain that Averroes devoted himself with such unflagging zeal to the composition of commentaries on the works of Aristotle that he became known among the Christian philosophers by the title of 'the commentator' (*Commentator*).

In his interpretation of Aristotle, Averroes, like Avicenna, was influenced by Neo-platonism, though his theory of creation was less coloured by the Neoplatonic idea of emanation. But the doctrine of Averroes which created the greatest excitement in the academic world of Western Christendom was that concerning the human intellect.

Aristotle had distinguished in man the active intellect, which 'abstracts' the forms or essences of things, from the passive or potential intellect which receives these forms as concepts or ideas. The scholastic philosophers commonly represented Averroes as saying that both the active and passive or potential intellects are separate intelligences which enter into a temporary connexion with individual human beings. But this interpretation is inaccurate, in so far as it implies that for Averroes the active and passive intellects are entirely distinct separate Intelligences. What he held was that the active intellect, which is one in all men, produces, through its contact with the individual passive intellect (which is a mere disposition to receive ideas), a kind of combination of the two, which he called the 'material' intellect. This latter is, however, no more than the particular activity of the separate active intellect in a definite individual. In any case the main point is that for Averroes there is only one intellectual principle which is immortal; and this principle is numerically one in all men, entering into a temporary connexion with individual beings as an illuminating activity. There is no individual intellect in man which survives death. Consequently there is no personal immortality. In so far as it is legitimate to speak of the individual's potential intellect as surviving death, it does so only as a moment in the life of the separate Intelligence.

This doctrine was not in harmony with orthodox Mohammedan theology. Averroes coped with this difficulty by saying that reason compelled him to assert the unicity of the intellect in all men, but that he held firmly to the contrary opinion by faith. What exactly he meant by this is not clear; and various interpretations of his mind have been given. What is clear, however, is that he interpreted Aristotle's cryptic remarks in the *De anima* in this way, and that he regarded Aristotle as the embodiment of reason, the culmination of human genius. We shall see that there arose in the faculty of arts at Paris a group of integral Aristotelians or 'Latin Averroists', as they have been called, who proposed the same monopsychistic doctrine as a necessary conclusion of reason. Needless to say, the theologian-philosophers, like St. Bonaventure and St. Thomas, were united in a common front against this doctrine, whatever their differences with one another on other points may have been. Nevertheless, the Christian philosophers had a profound respect for Averroes, and for the Islamic philosophers in general; and it is significant that Dante, in the *Divina Commedia*, places

Avicenna and Averroes in Limbo, and not in hell with Mohammed.

The Islamic philosophers were looked on with some suspicion by the orthodox Mohammedan theologians. Avicenna was strongly criticized by Algazel (1058–1111) for his doctrine of creation; and Averroes had to leave Spain owing to the suspicion and hostility aroused by his unorthodox philosophical opinions. In fact, the study of Greek philosophy was forbidden in Islamic Spain.

3. There were many Jews in Spain; and Jewish thinkers were naturally affected by the interest in Greek philosophy which was shown in the Islamic world. The two most prominent Jewish philosophers were Salomon Ibn Gabirol (c. 1021–69), known to the Christians, who thought that he was an Arab, as Avicebron, and Moses Maimonides (1135–1204). The former's *Fountain of Life*, originally composed in Arabic, had a considerable influence on Christian philosophers, though his thought was strongly coloured by Neo-platonism. Maimonides, who was born at Córdoba but died at Cairo, having had to leave Spain owing to the hostility shown towards the philosophers, was a closer adherent of Aristotle. On the other hand, he took pains to reconcile Aristotle with the Scriptures; and he exercised a positive influence on Aquinas through, for example, his proofs of God's existence. His general principle in regard to discrepancies between philosophy and Scriptural theology was as follows. When the teaching of the Old Testament on a certain point is clear, and when the philosophical arguments which can be advanced in favour of the contrary position are not so conclusive as to compel us to change our interpretation

of the Scriptures, we must accept what the Scripture teaches. We must, for example, reject Aristotle's opinion regarding the eternity of the world and of motion. When, however, reason plainly and conclusively shows that a statement of the Old Testament cannot be accepted in its *prima facie* sense, the statement must be given an allegorical interpretation. This was not a particularly revolutionary attitude; and it was in harmony with the teaching of Philo, the eminent Jewish philosopher of the ancient world; but it was too much for some of Maimonides' fellow Jews, who thought that he had sold the pass to the Greeks.

CHAPTER V

UNIVERSITIES: FRANCISCAN PHILOSOPHERS

1. IT is difficult to assign any definite date for the foundation of the older universities. In the year 1200 the university of Paris received a charter from Philip Augustus; and its statutes were approved by the Papal Legate, Robert de Courçon, in 1215. But to all intents and purposes the schools of Paris had coalesced into a 'university', in the sense of an institute of higher education possessing more than one faculty and open to scholars and students from elsewhere, in the second half of the twelfth century. Oxford was founded a little later than Paris, and Cambridge later than Oxford; but there were certainly schools at Oxford in the first half of the twelfth century, though the university was not formally constituted until later. The granting of a charter by papal or royal or imperial authority at a definite date certainly does not mean that in the case of the older medieval universities there was not already in existence what the medievals called a *studium generale* or centre of studies for students from different localities. The term *universitas* denoted, in the Middle Ages, the body of professors and students teaching and studying in a certain city; and the charter formally constituted them as a corporation, with definite statutes and privileges.

In the field of theology and speculative philosophy Paris was undoubtedly the most important university of the thirteenth century. The policy of the Holy See, especially of Popes Innocent III, who sanctioned the statutes through his legate, and Gregory IX, was to promote the service of religion and of the Church by the conciliation of philosophy with theology. In other words, Paris was regarded as the intellectual champion and bulwark of Christian truth. As for Bologna, the university of this city was also of great importance; but rather in the field of law, ecclesiastical and civil, than in that of dogmatic theology or of philosophy. It was at Paris that the contact between Christian theology and Greek and Islamic philosophy first led to momentous results. At Oxford the theologian-philosophers were markedly conservative in spirit, strongly attached to the Augustinian tradition, though this conservatism was combined with another trait, characteristic of the Oxford of the period, namely the cultivation of mathematics and science as transmitted by the Arabs. Roger Bacon is an excellent example of the fusion of the so-called Augustinian spirit with a lively interest and confidence in mathematics and empirical science.

One of the most important events in the life of the university of Paris, and indeed in that of other universities too, was the introduction of houses of study maintained by the new religious Orders. The Dominicans, as the Order of Preachers, were from the start friends of the study of theology; but St. Francis of Assisi with his enthusiastic idealism for the literal following of Christ and strict evangelical poverty, did not envisage members of his order devoting themselves to scholarship and learning. The Holy See, however, was quick to realize the potentialities of the new and fervent mendicant Orders; and Gregory IX in particular, who as cardinal had contributed to the development of study in the Franciscan order, did all he could to introduce the Dominicans and Franciscans into the life of the university of Paris and to maintain them there. In 1217 the Dominicans established themselves in Paris, and in 1229 they obtained a chair of theology. In the same year the Franciscans, who had established themselves at Paris a little later than the Dominicans, also obtained a chair, Alexander of Hales, an Englishman, being their first professor. Both Orders soon erected *studia generalia* (houses of study open to students from all provinces of the Order) in other universities, such as Oxford. And other religious Orders presently followed their example. The entry of the religious Orders into the university of Paris did not take place without a good deal of opposition from the secular clergy;[1] but the Dominicans and Franciscans enjoyed the support of the Holy See, and the opposition they met with, though vigorous, was overcome. The great majority of the well-known philosophers of the thirteenth century were members of religious Orders.

2. As has been mentioned already, the philosophical system of Aristotle, which had been made known to the Christian philosophers through the translations, could not possibly be ignored. On the other hand, it is understandable that it was not received with open arms by the theologians. Aristotle certainly taught the eternity of the world; and

---

[1] The term 'secular clergy' denotes those members of the clergy who do not belong to a religious Order. Those who do are called the 'regular clergy'.

this doctrine was in conflict with the theology of creation. What is more, he was presented by Averroes as a philosopher who denied personal immortality. To make matters worse, David of Dinant, who is stated by St. Thomas to have identified God and prime matter, appealed to the *Metaphysics* in support of his doctrine. If David really thought that Aristotle held a form of materialistic pantheism, he was, of course, mistaken; but that is another matter. In any case in 1210 the Provincial Council of Paris forbade the teaching of Aristotle's 'natural philosophy' in public or private; and when the statutes of the university were sanctioned in 1215 Aristotle's works on metaphysics and natural philosophy were prohibited, along with the doctrine of David of Dinant and certain other philosophers, one of whom ('Maurice of Spain') was probably Averroes. The study of the *Ethics* was not prohibited; nor, of course, were the logical works banned, some of which, as we have seen, had been known and utilized from the beginning of the Middle Ages. In 1231, Gregory IX appointed a commission of theologians to 'correct' the works of Aristotle, a measure which obviously implied that Aristotelianism was not considered fundamentally erroneous. The prohibitions were renewed in 1263; but they were of no effect. In the middle of the century, lectures were being given at Paris on all the known works of Aristotle. Moreover, as historians have pointed out, Urban IV must have been perfectly well aware that William of Moerbeke was translating Aristotle at his own court. Probably the pope aimed at checking the spread of 'Averroism' rather than at stifling all study of Aristotle. In any case, whatever Urban IV may have intended,

Aristotelianism had already begun its vigorous life in the Christian medieval world.

3. It is possible to divide the different currents of thought in the thirteenth century according to the various attitudes adopted towards Aristotelianism. To do this would doubtless constitute an over-simplification and would result in one-sided presentation of thirteenth-century thought, were one to pretend that this treatment of the subject is comprehensive and entirely adequate. But to interpret the different currents of thought in the light of the various attitudes adopted in regard to Aristotelianism has at least this advantage, that it enables one to form an intelligible picture, with clear lines, of the development of philosophy in that period and of the conflicts which arose. The picture may not be adequate; but to paint a completely adequate picture on such a small canvas as that presented by the present volume would scarcely be possible. Anyone acquainted with the history of philosophy is aware of the difficulty of attaining anything like a definitive interpretation of the development of thought in a given period; and the Middle Ages certainly do not constitute an exception.

The thinkers of what is generally called the 'Augustinian tradition' were reserved in their attitude towards Aristotle. They certainly utilized the philosophy of Aristotle in varying degrees; but I see no particular advantage to be gained in calling them 'incomplete Aristotelians' simply because they adopted certain ideas from Aristotle but did not go so far in their utilization of Aristotle as St. Thomas did. Take St. Bonaventure, for example. Born in 1221, he became a Franciscan and studied at Paris under Alexander of Hales. He subsequently taught in the university until he was elected General of his Order in 1257. He died in 1274, the same year as St. Thomas, being then bishop of Albano and a cardinal. On some matters he agreed with Aristotle. For instance, in his view of the way in which the mind acquires knowledge of sensible things, namely in dependence on sensation and without possessing any innate ideas, he was more or less at one with Aristotle. He spoke in a similar way about our knowledge of 'primary principles'. Nobody apprehends the general principle that the whole is greater than the part until he has learnt by experience what 'whole' and 'part' mean or are. Once he has learnt by experience of some sort what the words mean, that is, once he has acquired the ideas, the natural light of the intellect enables him to see the truth of the general proposition. He possesses no 'innate' actual knowledge of the general proposition or principle; and there is no reason for calling 'innate' a knowledge which is acquired in dependence on experience. On this point St. Bonaventure was in agreement with Aristotle, and also with St. Thomas. Again, St. Bonaventure certainly thought in terms of categories which were Aristotelian in character; for example, substance and accident. But so did all other medieval philosophers of the thirteenth century. Moreover, the Aristotelian categories were known and employed by Christian theologians and philosophers long before the thirteenth century. They were to be found, for example, in Boethius. The use of them makes St. Bonaventure an 'Aristotelian' in some sense, it is true. He used the Aristotelian logic; and his metaphysics and cosmology were partially Aristotelian in character. So we can, if we wish, call him an 'incomplete Aristotelian'. But this does not alter the fact that his attitude towards Aristotle considered as a metaphysician was by no means one of unqualified friendliness; and his sympathies, expressed in the spirit of his philosophy, were with Augustine, not with Aristotle. It will be worth while to illustrate this spirit briefly, as St. Bonaventure is an outstanding example of the conservative theologian-philosopher who took his stand with 'the common opinions of the masters', that is to say, with the opinions of his Christian predecessors.

In St. Bonaventure's eyes Aristotle was a gifted natural philosopher, who rightly refused to regard the sensible world as no fit object for knowledge. But he was wrong in rejecting Plato's archetypal Forms or 'Ideas'; and the reasons he adduced in the *Metaphysics* for this rejection 'are valueless'. Plato saw that the sensible world stands to transcendent reality in the relation of copy to model. This is the doctrine of exemplarism; and exemplarism is the key and centre of metaphysics. It follows that Aristotle was no true metaphysician. If we seek the full truth about exemplarism, we have to turn from Plato to Augustine; but Plato did at least discern a truth which Aristotle failed to grasp. Moreover, if there are no divine ideas and if God, as Aristotle thought, is simply the final cause of movement, there can be no creative activity on God's part. It is no wonder, then, that Aristotle rejected creation and taught the eternity of the world. In St. Bonaventure's opinion, though not in that of St. Thomas, this last notion, that of the eternity of the world, is, in itself, a demonstrably absurd notion. For example, if the

world had existed from eternity, that is, if time had
had no beginning, an infinite series would already
have been traversed, which is impossible. Moreover,
it would be possible to add to the infinite, which is
also absurd. The arguments adduced by St. Bonaventure may not be cogent; but it is clear that he
did not simply confront Aristotle's doctrine of the
eternity of the world with theological doctrine and
leave it at that.

But it was not simply that St. Bonaventure rejected various particular doctrines of Aristotle. He
did indeed make a formal distinction between theology and philosophy. Theology starts with the data
of revelation and applies reason in the attempt to
understand them, whereas philosophy starts with the
world about us and argues to God as cause. But in
his own metaphysics of exemplarism the influence of
the Christian faith is not only clear but also acknowledged. Every creature is a 'vestige of God' or 'a
shadow of God'; but the rational creature is the
'image of God' in a special sense. As Bonaventure
links this doctrine of exemplarism and the accompanying theory of analogy with a doctrine of the
spiritual life of man, it might seem that he is talking
pure theology. Man's spiritual ascent means a turning from the 'shadow' or more remote likeness to the
'image of God', and from the image to the exemplary
cause itself, that is, to God. But, apart from the fact
that a doctrine of man's spiritual ascent is found in
some philosophies of the ancient world, as in that of
Plotinus, it is important to bear in mind Bonaventure's conviction that exemplarism is the heart of
metaphysics and that metaphysics is necessarily
unsatisfactory unless it is linked up with theology.

For the natural philosopher the world is simply 'nature'; and he considers it in itself, without reference to any but a physical relation to God, like that of thing moved to its mover. The metaphysician, however, considers the world as also a manifestation of God and ascends to a knowledge of the divine ideas and of God as creative and exemplary cause. But, unless it is realized that the divine ideas, which are not ontologically distinct from one another, exist in the Word of God, as Augustine realized, the metaphysician stops short of the full truth. More than that, unless he philosophizes in the light of faith, he will certainly fall into error. For example, the philosopher can arrive at the truth of the unity of God. But unless he accepts the revealed doctrine of the Trinity he will assert the divine unity in such a way as not only to prescind from but also to exclude the trinity of Persons. The philosopher as such cannot prove the dogma of the Trinity, which is a revealed mystery; but if he lacks the light of faith he will leave no room, as it were, for the Trinity. Hence, though philosophy and theology are formally distinct, the metaphysician will certainly err unless he carries on his activity in the light of faith. In this sense theology and metaphysics are closely allied.

St. Bonaventure's interest, then, always centred round man's relation and orientation to God. This interest shows itself, for example, in the arguments he uses to prove God's existence. He does, indeed, employ arguments for the existence of God as first cause and as necessary being, as well as Augustine's argument from eternal truths; but he also believed that by reflecting on his desire for happiness man can come to the explicit knowledge of God, since the desire for happiness is the desire for the possession of a complete and absolute good; and this is, in the concrete, God. Indeed, the orientation of the will towards the possession of the supreme good manifests an initial dim and implicit awareness of God's existence. Similarly, in order to show that the soul is immortal, Bonaventure argued from the immaterial nature of the soul; but his favourite argument was based on the soul's desire for perfect and enduring happiness. Finally, though he accepted the Aristotelian account of abstraction, he did not think that it is sufficient to explain human knowledge. We could not apprehend the intelligible and unchanging merely through mental abstraction from sensible things: we need the regulative and guiding action of the divine light. Aristotle was unable to see the necessity for divine illumination, but St. Augustine realized that we cannot attain unchanging truth without the light of the divine Word. The Word is operative within every man, even if he is unaware of it.

Owing to the stress he lays on exemplarism and on illumination St. Bonaventure's philosophy may well be called 'Augustinian'. And owing to the way in which he links up these themes with the theological theme of man's ascent to God through Christ, the divine Word, it may well be called a 'Christian philosophy'. He had a unified view of reality, elaborated in the light of his Christian faith; and, though he certainly adopted and utilized Aristotelian ideas, he regarded Aristotle himself as a natural philosopher rather than as a metaphysician. It is quite clear that he mistrusted any tendency to accept the whole Aristotelian system as if it were 'Philosophy' itself.

In the thirteenth century the Franciscan thinkers, were, for the most part, conservatives. This showed itself in their maintenance of various theories which were characteristic of the Augustinian tradition. For example, they maintained that divine illumination of the human intellect is necessary in order to explain human knowledge of 'eternal truths'. This certainly was an Augustinian doctrine; and in regard to it one must remember two things. First, divine illumination was not postulated simply in order to explain mystical experience: it was postulated in order to explain the apprehension of the necessary and immutable elements in the judgement. One can say, I suppose, in other language, that it was postulated in order to explain our apprehension of analytic propositions, and of synthetic *a priori* propositions, in so far as the *a priori* element of the latter is concerned. As I have remarked before, its function corresponded in some degree to the function of reminiscence in Plato. Secondly, those who maintained the theory of divine illumination did not mean to imply that our ideas either of sensible objects or of ideas derived from sensible objects are infused by God. They did not reject the Aristotelian psychology and epistemology altogether: what they thought was that the doctrine of abstraction is not sufficient to explain even normal human knowledge in all its aspects.

It was only natural that the spread of Aristotelianism in the thirteenth century and its utilization by Aquinas should have an effect on the Franciscan philosophers; and that their traditionally conservative attitude should undergo modification. For example, Richard of Middleton, an English Franciscan who died about the end of the thirteenth century, declared that it was quite unnecessary to postulate any special divine illumination, as our philosophic knowledge not only of the nature of corporeal beings but also of spiritual beings can be explained quite well without it. And with Duns Scotus, whose philosophy will be considered later, we find an original synthesis, which was elaborated under the influence of Aristotelianism and of Islamic philosophy and which bears the stamp of a powerful and creative mind. On the other hand we find uncompromising traditionalists like the Franciscan Roger Marston (d. 1303), who insisted on what he regarded as the Augustinian theory of divine illumination, identified the illuminating active intellect with God, and declared that one ought to prefer the 'saints', like Augustine and Anselm, to those 'infernal men', the pagan philosphers.

A more interesting figure, however, is Roger Bacon (about 1212 to after 1292), also an English Franciscan. In some respects he adhered to the Augustinian tradition and outlook. He maintained, for example, the theories of divine illumination, of germinal forms, and of the 'form of corporeity'.[1] But he was a man of independent, and indeed somewhat intolerant, mind. He studied at Oxford under the famous Robert Grosseteste (d. 1253), whom he praises for his knowledge of mathematics and perspective. But for most of the professors whom he encountered at Paris he had little respect. He had a hearty dislike for the deference they paid to great

[1] The traditional theory was that the human body, for example, is constituted as one body by the form of corporeity. At death the soul is separated from the body; but the body remains the same body, by virtue of the form of corporeity, until corruption takes place.

names and to the opinions of their predecessors. Indeed, the first cause of human ignorance which he lists in his *Opus maius,* is subjection to authority which does not merit it. Aristotle, he observes, recognized this fact. One may as well remark perhaps that when Roger Bacon fulminates against subjection to authority he is not thinking of acceptance of the Christian dogmas, but of quoting the opinions of other philosophers as solutions to problems. But what particularly annoyed him in his contemporaries was their ignorance of the sciences and of languages. Mathematics has fallen into neglect among the Latins, he says. And, as to languages, how can the Scriptures and the Greek and Arabic philosophers be properly translated and interpreted without a good knowledge of the appropriate languages?

Robert Grosseteste had insisted on the need for observation and experiment in the study of nature, and Roger Bacon followed him in this insistence. Although Bacon depended to a great extent on the work of Greek and Arabic writers, he made his own observations, in the field of optics, for example, and urged observation on others. He was also quick to see the practical purposes to which scientific knowledge could be put. He conceived, for instance, the possibility of the telescope. Moreover, both Grosseteste and Bacon laid great emphasis on the role of mathematics in science. We have to start with the empirical data; but the aim of theoretical science is to render the data intelligible; and they are made intelligible by being explained deductively in the light of mathematical reasoning. 'Experience' is necessary in order to become acquainted with the empirical data and to extend one's factual knowledge and also in order to confirm the conclusions of deductive reasoning from 'causes' ascertained by induction; but a mere accumulation of empirical data does not constitute science.

It would be wrong to give or to attempt to give the impression that thirteenth-century universities were peopled with students of science in the modern sense; but it would also be wrong to give the impression that the first steps in empirical science and in understanding scientific method were taken in the fourteenth century, in connexion with the Ockhamist movement. Grosseteste and Witelo, a thirteenth-century Silesian physicist and philosopher, studied refraction. Bacon gave his attention to optics; and others, like Jordanus Nemorarius, a Dominican, made discoveries in mechanics. And one should not forget that Aristotle himself had taught that we have to begin with the empirical data: his own interest in the observation of biological facts is well enough known. Grosseteste and Bacon were both influenced by the writings of the Greek philosopher: they did not regard their scientific interest as being in contradiction with his teaching. At the same time they developed the Aristotelian ideas. Aristotle had held that we have scientific knowledge in the proper sense only when we can show that the effects follow necessarily from 'causes' as conclusion follow from premisses in logic; but he had given no clear indication how the knowledge of such 'causes' is to be obtained in physical science. Bacon, however, tried to show how the 'cause' of the facts can be ascertained by eliminating explanatory theories which are incompatible with the facts. In other words, he had some grasp of the importance of hypothesis in science and of the role of verification in confirming or discrediting a given hypothesis. Thirteenth-century science was certainly primitive and elementary; but research has shown, first that some of the scientific theories and investigations of the Renaissance were anticipated in the fourteenth century, and secondly that four-teenth-century science was not entirely a new development but had its roots in the preceding century.

The mind of Bacon was somewhat complex. A man of firm faith and, in regard to a number of philo-sophical theories, a conservative of the Augustinian school, he yet combined a real respect for Aristotle, Seneca, Averroes, and other non-Christian philo-sophers with an emphasis on independence of judge-ment and a lively sense of the importance of the sciences. When he is speaking of experience and the value of experiment in the sixth part of the *Opus Maius* he divides experience into sense-experience and experience of spiritual things, which, with the aid of divine grace, may attain the heights of mysti-cism. This combination of a spiritual outlook with a belief in the value of the sciences was not indeed un-characteristic of medieval Oxford; but in the thir-teenth century it was Roger Bacon above all who attained a grasp of the nature of scientific method, with its combination of deduction and induction, in so far, that is, as it was possible to apprehend the nature of scientific method in an age when physical science was very little developed.

CHAPTER VI

ST. THOMAS AQUINAS

1. THE man who really attempted to weld the philosophical system of Aristotle and Christian theology
into a harmonious whole was the Dominican friar,
St. Thomas Aquinas. Looking back at the medieval
scene across the centuries which have elapsed since
St. Thomas lived and wrote, one is apt to forget that
he was an innovator and that he seemed to his contemporaries an 'advanced' thinker. One is apt to
think to oneself perhaps: 'Medieval philosophy?—
Oh yes, Aristotle!' The fact is, however, that by
lending his full, though not uncritical support, to the
Aristotelian philosophy, the scope of which had only
recently become known, Aquinas not only immensely
enriched Christian thought but also took a bold step.
We have already seen how the metaphysical and
cosmological works of Aristotle had been prohibited
at Paris. Whatever may be thought of some later
Christian Aristotelians, the levelling of any accusation of 'obscurantism' against Aquinas would betray
a complete misunderstanding of the situation in the
first half of the thirteenth century. On the other
hand, Aquinas did not simply embrace Aristotelianism because it was novel, he embraced it because he
thought it was in the main true, though he certainly
did not regard Aristotle as infallible.

St. Thomas was born at the end of 1224 or beginning of 1225 at Roccasecca near Naples. His
father was the Count of Aquino. St. Thomas entered

the Dominican Order in 1244 and went to Paris in 1245. His life was spent in studying and teaching, mainly at Paris, though he was also for a time at the papal court. Apart from some excitement in his youth, when his family kidnapped him and tried to prevent his persisting in his resolution to be a Dominican, he led the life of a university professor: indeed, he possessed some of the characteristics traditionally associated with professors, such as absent-mindedness. Patient, thorough, open-minded, and fair, he was free from all fanaticism and he never regarded abuse as an adequate substitute for reasoned argument and discussion. A 'rationalist' in the best sense of the word, he was also a saint, who at any rate towards the close of his life enjoyed mystical experience of God. He died on the 7th of March 1274, when on his way from Naples to take part in the Second Council of Lyons.

As a student Thomas had been in close contact with a remarkable man, St. Albert the Great (1206–80), a German Dominican who taught at Paris and Cologne. Albert's philosophy had a rather eclectic character, combining theories taken from traditional Augustinianism and from Neo-platonism, as represented by the *Liber de causis*, with genuine Aristotelianism. But it was he who opened the mind of his pupil, Thomas Aquinas, to the value and significance of the Aristotelian philosophy, which he explained in his lectures and writings. In addition, Albert the Great had a strong and lively interest in empirical research and a robust confidence in the value of observation and verification. In his works on plants and animals he did not rely simply on the statements of previous writers, but gave the results of his own observations, so far as he had been able to make them, insisting that in matters of this kind knowledge depends on empirical observation. In his speculations on scientific matters he gave evidence of common sense and of a dislike of jumping to hasty conclusions. (There are, incidentally, stories about his own inventions.) But, though he exercised a strong formative influence on the mind of Aquinas, he apparently did not bequeath to his pupil his own omnivorous curiosity and passion for empirical research. Albert did not possess Thomas's genius for systematization; and the latter did not share the former's bent for scientific inquiries. One cannot do everything, to be sure.

2. In the first chapter I said that Aquinas gave a clear statement of the methodic difference between philosophy and theology. That he took this distinction seriously can be shown by an example. He was convinced that the arguments brought by a thinker like St. Bonaventure to show that motion and time must have had a beginning were not conclusive. According to Thomas, no philosopher had ever succeeded in proving conclusively that creation from eternity is impossible and that motion and time must therefore have had a beginning. The philosopher, then, must suspend judgement on the matter. On the other hand, theology teaches that time had a beginning. In other words, we know by revelation a truth which the philosopher can discuss but which he has never succeeded in proving. This does not mean, of course, that the philosopher can prove the opposite of what theology clearly teaches: if Thomas rejected Bonaventure's arguments to prove that motion and time must have had a beginning, he also

rejected Aristotle's arguments to show that they cannot have had a beginning. Thomas may have had a profound admiration for Aristotle, but he did not regard an argument as sound simply because Aristotle used it, or a statement as true simply because Aristotle made it. One may or may not agree with Thomas's Aristotelianism; but there is no reason for regarding him as an uncritical worshipper at Aristotle's shrine. On the contrary, he profoundly modified Aristotelianism, not only in the light of the Christian religion and the teaching of the Fathers, but also in the light of his own reflections.

3. Perhaps the easiest way to give some idea of Aquinas's philosophy is to start by outlining his analysis of those corporeal things which form the immediate object of our normal experience. In this analysis one can distinguish various levels, as it were. First of all, Thomas accepted the traditional Aristotelian doctrine of substance and accident. The actual size or the colour of a goat, for example, is an accidental modification: it can change while the goat remains the same substance. But let us suppose that the goat is killed and eaten by a lion. That which was goat flesh receives, when digested by the lion, another substantial determination or 'form'; it is now 'informed' by the form of the lion. In every corporeal substance we can distinguish the 'matter' and the 'form'. And if we think away all determining principles or 'forms' we can conceive, though only by a process of negation, a purely potential principle, which is capable of receiving, though only successively, all bodily forms. In every corporeal substance we can distinguish, then, what Aristotle called 'first matter', the potential principle, and substantial

form, the determining principle which makes a thing the kind of thing it is.

The distinction between substance and accident was well known to the medievals from the beginning, while the hylomorphic theory (matter and form) made its appearance at Chartres in the twelfth century, as has already been noted. Both the substance-accident theory and the hylomorphic theory were Aristotelian. So also was the distinction between act and potency or potentiality. Following Aristotle, Aquinas saw in all finite substances, whether corporeal or not, both the capability of receiving further perfections or modifications and the determining principle which makes the thing what it is or becomes. Composition from matter and form is but one instance, confined to corporeal substances, of the distinction between potentiality and act: the matter is in potentiality to the reception of form, and form stands to the matter as act to potentiality. But in spiritual beings too, the distinction between act and potentiality obtains. An angel, for instance, is capable of making acts of love or of receiving divine illumination or grace. The distinction between act and potentiality is thus more fundamental and pervasive than that between matter and form. It is, moreover, a mark of limitation and finiteness: a thing is capable of change or of receiving a further perfection or determination because it is limited or finite or imperfect. God, who is pure act and absolute perfection, cannot change or receive further perfection: the absolutely perfect being simply *is*: it cannot become.

Now, I do not mean to suggest that the foregoing analysis of corporeal substance in particular and of

finite being in general is peculiarly Thomist. It is
Aristotelian in origin, and it is found in other medieval
philosophers, in Bonaventure, for example. But
Aquinas carried the analysis of finite being a stage
further than Aristotle by distinguishing between
essence and existence in every finite being. A finite
being or substance has or possesses existence; and its
existence is an act in relation to its essence or nature.
In other words, it is not of the essence of any finite
being to exist: its existence is received and limited by
its essence. But existence and essence are not two
separable things: nor does essence first have being
and then receive existence. To say this would be to
affirm a contradiction in terms. Essence and existence are the two ultimate constitutive, metaphysical
principles of every finite thing. This essence-existence language is certainly extremely unfashionable
today in British philosophical circles; but there can
be no doubt of the importance which Aquinas
attached to this analysis of finite being, even though
the precise nature of the distinction which he meant to
assert between essence and existence has been, and
still is, matter for dispute. The essence-existence
distinction was not altogether a novelty. As we have
seen, it was recognized by Avicenna, though he
tended to make existence an accident; and it passed
into scholastic philosophy with William of Auvergne.
But it was Aquinas who first attached to it a profound importance. Through this analysis the dependence of every finite thing is revealed. And this at
once raises the problem of God. Perhaps it is as well
to remark at once that, for Aquinas, there is in God
no distinction between essence and existence. God's
existence and essence are identical: his essence is

existence. And this is what Aquinas means when he speaks of God as the 'necessary being'.

4. Aquinas, in the *Summa Theologica*, gives five ways of proving God's existence. First he argues from the fact of motion (which does not mean simply locomotion, but, as with Aristotle, the reduction of potentiality to act) to the existence of a first mover. This argument is based on Aristotle's argument in the *Metaphysics*. Secondly, he argues that there must be a first efficient cause; and, thirdly, that there must be a necessary being. We see that there are at any rate some beings which do not necessarily exist, for there are beings which begin to be and cease to be. But, these beings (contingent beings) would not exist, if they were the only type of being; for they are dependent for their existence. Ultimately there must exist a being which exists necessarily and is not dependent. The fourth argument proceeds from degrees of perfection observed in the world to the existence of a supreme or perfect being; and the fifth argument, based on the finality in the corporeal world, concludes with asserting the existence of God as cause of finality and order in the world. In these proofs the idea of dependence is fundamental, being successively applied to the observed facts of motion, efficient causality, coming into being and passing away, degrees of finite perfections, and lastly finality. None of the proofs were entirely new; nor did Aquinas think they were new. He was not writing for atheists but was engaged in showing the rational foundation of faith as a preliminary to treating of theological matters. The only proof which he develops at any length (in the *Summa contra Gentiles*) is the first, namely that from motion.

I do not propose to discuss the validity of St. Thomas's arguments; but there are several explanatory remarks which ought to be made. First of all, when he talks about a 'first' mover or a 'first' cause, he does not mean first in the temporal order. This is quite clear from the fact that he did not admit that the philosopher can prove the impossibility of a series of created things going back infinitely, or indefinitely, into the past. By 'first' he means 'supreme' or 'ultimate'. His point is that the series, whether finite or infinite, itself requires an ultimate explanation. Therefore, secondly, when he speaks about the impossibility of an 'infinite regress' in, for example, the series of efficient causes, he is referring to an infinite regress not in the temporal order but in the order of ontological dependence. What he means can be expressed in this way. An infinite regress of contingent beings, for example, is not an explanation of the existence of those beings; it is impossible in the sense that without a 'necessary being' the series, whether temporally finite or infinite, would not exist. To bring in the idea of an infinite regress as if it were an explanation does not help matters: that is the point he wants to make. Thirdly, it is perfectly true that Aquinas presupposes as metaphysical principles the principles of sufficient reason and of causality; but so did his contemporaries. We shall see later that the validity of the traditional proofs of God's existence were questioned in the fourteenth century. Whether Aquinas and his fellow metaphysicians or their fourteenth-century critics were right or wrong is a question which the historian need not discuss. But it is important to realize that Aquinas regarded a principle like that of sufficient reason as being not simply a 'logical' principle in the sense in which 'logical principle' is sometimes understood today, that is, as a purely formal principle or 'tautology', but as a metaphysical principle, stating a 'law' of being.

It might, of course, be asked with what justification Aquinas calls the first mover or the necessary being 'God'. But he goes on, of course, to show that the 'necessary being' must have the attributes which we predicate of God. For example, he argues that the supreme being must be intelligent. Now, this raises the question of the meaning of the terms we predicate of God; and this question is rendered all the more acute by Aquinas's psychology and epistemology. For Aquinas not only accepted the Aristotelian view of the human soul as the 'form' of the body, but he also maintained that human knowledge depends on sense-perception. The soul is not in the body like a pilot in a ship; it is naturally united to the body, their union not being something artificial. And this truth expresses itself in and is revealed by the fact that the first object of human knowledge is material reality. How, then, can the human mind attain the knowledge even of the existence of a spiritual being like God? Aquinas's reply is, in substance, that the human mind, which has as its primary object of knowledge the essences of corporeal things, can recognize the relation of the objects of experience to that on which they are dependent. It is, therefore, justified in affirming the existence of the being on which the things that form the world are dependent. But in regard to the nature of that being the human mind can know it only in so far as it is revealed in finite things. In a famous phrase, we know of God *that* He is rather than *what* He is.

Even so, to predicate any terms of God raises a problem. For the terms denote primarily experienced qualities or perfections. For example, the word 'intelligence' denotes primarily the intelligence of which we have experience, namely human intelligence. In what sense is it predicated of God? When we say that God is intelligent, we do not mean simply that God is the cause of human intelligence. If this were all that we meant, we might just as well say that God is matter. When we predicate of God those perfections which are compatible with infinite being, we mean more than that God is the cause of those perfections. But we cannot mean that God is intelligent in precisely the same way that a man is intelligent: we cannot, that is, be using the term in a univocal sense. Nor can we be using it purely equivocally. If we were, the term would have no meaning when applied to a being transcending our natural experience. We use the term, Aquinas says, analogically. We predicate of God something positive to which human intelligence bears some resemblance; but that resemblance is accompanied always by dissimilarity, and we can have no adequate knowledge of the reality which is affirmed. The philosopher can discover which terms can legitimately be predicated of God and which cannot; and he can approximate towards a knowledge of the objective meaning of those terms by trying to purify his concepts; but he cannot comprehend the full objective meaning of those terms. There is, then, in Thomas's philosophy a certain 'agnosticism'; but it is a partial agnosticism, resulting from a conviction of the divine transcendence on the one hand and the limitations of the human mind and of language on the other hand, not

from indifference or from a despair of ever finding out
anything at all about God.

5. It has been pointed out that Thomas accepted
the Aristotelian doctrine that the soul is the form of
the body. It is the one rational soul of man which
makes the human body a human body, and which is
the principle of its vital functions and of sensation.
But, once given this conception of the relation of
soul to body, it might seem that a grave difficulty
arises in regard to immortality. If the soul is naturally the form of the body, must it not perish at death,
like the sensitive soul of an animal? St. Thomas
answers that the rational soul, although the form of
the body, must be a spiritual or immaterial form.
That it transcends matter can be known by an in-
spection of its activities; for it is capable of knowing
all kinds of bodies and is not confined to a restricted
field in the same way that the power of vision is confined to the perception of objects as coloured. The
mind can know material essences, and it can, in
addition, reflect on itself. It must, therefore, be
immaterial. But the existence of an immaterial form
is not intrinsically dependent on the matter which it
informs. Aquinas drew the conclusion from the
Aristotelian doctrine of the soul that the disembodied
soul is not, properly speaking, a 'person'. The person
is, as Boethius defined it, an individual substance of
rational nature; and the body is a part of man, who
is himself a complete substance. Nevertheless, the
soul, being an immaterial principle, survives bodily
death. As to the Aristotelian doctrine as interpreted
by Averroes, that immortality belongs only to the
separate active intellect which is one in all men,
St. Thomas refused to admit that the doctrine has

any real foundation in experience. The intellectual life of one man differs from that of another man as much as one man's sensations differ from those of another man. Each man has his own active intellect; and immortality is personal immortality.

6. The combination of Aristotelianism with a philosophy inspired by a Christian outlook is very clear in St. Thomas's moral doctrine. He accepted the eudaemonism and teleology of the Aristotelian ethic, in the sense that he accepted the Aristotelian doctrine that happiness is the end of human life and that the goodness or badness of actions depends on their relation to this end. In this sense he accepted the primary of the good in the moral life. But, apart from the fact that St. Thomas understood by happiness, the end of human life, a good which is perfectly attainable only in the next life, he linked up ethics and metaphysics in a way that Aristotle had not done. But the association of ethics with metaphysics in Aquinas's philosophy has to be carefully understood. The notion that the moral law depends on the arbitrary choice or enactment of God is quite foreign to the mind of Aquinas. His position was rather as follows. From eternity God had in His mind, to speak anthropomorphically, an idea of human nature. He saw the acts required for the attainment of the end of that nature, that is, for the full development of its potentialities. This plan for man is the eternal law; but it does not depend on divine caprice. Human nature is one way in which the divine essence can be externally reflected; and, given human nature, there are certain acts which are required for the development of its potentialities and certain acts which are incompatible with that

development. The moral law is thus ultimately based on the necessary and changeless divine essence itself. As seen and approved by the divine intellect (again, this is anthropomorphic language, but this language is inevitable) it is the eternal law. This eternal law of God is reflected in the natural law, which is the totality of the dictates of man's practical reason concerning the good which is to be sought and the evil which is to be avoided. The natural law is immediately promulgated by the human reason itself, and in this sense man enjoys a certain moral autonomy. But human nature is always essentially the same; and so the natural law is always essentially the same. Therefore neither the ultimate transcendent foundation of the natural moral law nor its promulgation by the practical reason means that the natural law is arbitrary or could be otherwise than it is. Human reason promulgates the law through reflection on human nature. The moral imperative is thus, in Kantian language, an assertoric hypothetical imperative, though the scholastic philosopher would not like the use of the word 'hypothetical'. Obligation is the binding of the free will, as free, to perform that act which is necessary for the attainment of the last end; and this end, happiness, is absolute, in the sense that the will cannot help desiring it. When it comes to interpreting what this end is in the concrete, its character must be determined by reference to human nature. The moral law is not purely formal, but possesses a necessary content, determined by human nature.

7. This theory of natural law has important consequences in regard to human positive law, the law of the State. The function of human positive law is to

define and clarify the natural law and make it explicit, to apply it and to make it effective by the establishment of sanctions. The law of the State should define murder, for instance, and establish sanctions which will contribute to the observance of its enactments. This is not to say that the law of the State should contain enactments about every transgression of the natural law; for the former exists for the good of the community, and it may not be for the good of the community that an infringement of the natural law through this or that type of action should be taken cognisance of and punished by the law of the State. But it does mean that every legislative enactment of the State must be at any rate in harmony with the natural law. If a human positive law is incompatible with the natural law, says St. Thomas, it will be a perversion of law rather than a true law. It will be an unjust law, and it will not bind in conscience. That, of course, is an extreme case. It is also possible for the legislator to enact a law simply and solely for his own private and selfish interest; and such a law, even if it is not incompatible with the natural law as far as its content is concerned, will not bind in conscience, except in cases where non-observance of the law would produce a greater evil than that produced by observing a law which, though not intrinsically evil, is superfluous and not required for the common good. This conception of law follows from St. Thomas's definition of law as 'an ordinance of reason for the common good, made by him who has care of the community, and promulgated'.

For very many people today 'law' means the law of the State. For St. Thomas. however. the law of the

State is simply one kind of law. The word 'law', as a general term, includes the eternal law of God, the natural law, the divine positive law (the revealed law), and human positive law. Ultimately, all law derives its authority from God, and thus possesses a transcendent foundation. A good deal of this medieval conception of law is to be found in the philosophy of law of Richard Hooker (1553–1600), the English Protestant writer; and through Hooker it influenced John Locke, at least in regard to the moral character of human law and its relation to natural law. The later positivistic conception of law stands, of course, at the opposite pole to Aquinas's idea of law.

8. The esteem in which Aquinas, as theologian and philosopher, is now held in the Catholic Church may lead one to suppose that he occupied a similar position in the Middle Ages. But some of his theories were considered dangerous innovations by a certain number of his contemporaries. In 1277, three years after Aquinas's death, a number of propositions were condemned by the bishop of Paris; and though the condemnation was chiefly aimed at the 'Averroists', certain theories of Aquinas were included. In the same year the Dominican archbishop of Canterbury, Richard Kilwardby, condemned a set of propositions at Oxford, including Aquinas's theory of the unicity of the substantial form in the individual substance.[1] And in 1284 John Peckham, Kilwardby's Franciscan

---

[1] Aquinas maintained that in the human being, for example, there is only one substantial form, namely the rational soul, which directly informs 'first matter'. There is no 'form of corporeity', and still less are there distinct vegetative and sensitive souls or substantial forms, corresponding to the vital principles in plants and animals respectively.

successor in the See of Canterbury, repeated the condemnation. The reason why the traditionalists objected to Thomas's theory that in any substance there is only one substantial form was theological in character. If the soul of Christ, they thought, was the one substantial form of the body of Christ, and if there was no 'form of corporeity', it would follow that between Christ's death and resurrection His body was not really His body at all. In addition they considered that, on Thomas's theory, the veneration of the bodies and relics of saints could not be justified. Thomas had been of a different opinion; but his critics thought that his rejection of the traditional doctrine of a 'form of corporeity' was a perilous novelty.

After Aquinas's canonization in 1323 these attacks were naturally greatly modified; and two years later the bishop of Paris withdrew the censures of 1277. But though St. Thomas gradually came to be the official Doctor of the Dominican Order, he never became during the Middle Ages in any sense the official Catholic philosopher. It is incorrect to say that even now Thomism as such is officially imposed on all Catholic philosophers; but it is undeniable that since the encyclical letter *Aeterni Patris* of Pope Leo XIII, St. Thomas enjoys a status in the Catholic Church which has not been accorded to any other philosopher.

CHAPTER VII

THE AVERROISTS

ST. ALBERT THE GREAT, St. Thomas Aquinas, and
St. Bonaventure were all theologians and lectured in
the faculty of theology of the university of Paris. It
was the theologians who first interested themselves
in and employed the metaphysical works of Aristotle
and who saw the importance of the newly received
philosophical literature. But from about the middle
of the thirteenth century the professors and lecturers of the faculty of arts at Paris (or, rather, a
group of those professors and lecturers) began to give
their attention not only to the logical works of
Aristotle, as had formerly been the case in the faculty
of arts, but also to his metaphysical, cosmological, and
ethical writings. Doubtless their interest had been
aroused by the attention paid to Aristotle in the
theological faculty. In any case the activity of the
theologians in this respect helped to focus the attention of their colleagues of the faculty of arts on the
Aristotelian system as a whole.

But a big difference in attitude and method soon
showed itself between the members of the two
faculties. A theologian-philosopher like Albert or
Thomas was not inclined to take over Aristotelianism without modification; for it was quite obvious to
him that some of Aristotle's theories were incompatible with orthodox Christian theology, especially
if Averroes's commentaries were regarded as giving
the true interpretation of Aristotle's philosophy.
But a group of lecturers appeared in the faculty of

100

arts who were quite prepared to take over Aristotelianism as a whole without worrying their heads
whether all the theories asserted by Aristotle were
theologically orthodox or not. And some of them at
least did not hesitate to accept Averroes's commentaries as giving the right interpretation of Aristotle,
particularly in regard to the unicity of the intellect
in all members of the human species. Hence the
name commonly given to them, 'Averroists'.

A superficial view of the situation might lead some
people to the following conclusion. The theologians,
holding preconceived opinions, naturally had to dis-
tort Aristotle in order to fit him in with those
opinions. The professors of the faculty of arts, on
the other hand, were less prejudiced. They vindi-
cated the freedom and autonomy of philosophy in
face of the tyranny of theology. But an interpretation
of this kind would imply a radical misunderstanding
of the situation. In the first place, quite apart from
the question whether the Christian doctrines are true
or not, the theologian-philosophers, by the very fact
that they had to modify Aristotelianism if they chose
to accept it, were compelled to re-think critically the
Aristotelian theories and arguments. And it is a
matter of historical fact that the constructive efforts
in philosophy during the thirteenth century came
from the theologian-philosophers, not from the members of the faculty of arts. It was the latter, not the
theologians, who tended to regard the mind of
Aristotle as the embodiment of Reason and the culmination of human genius, and to equate philosophy
with Aristotelianism.

It is owing to the last fact that some historians
have maintained that the name 'Averroists' is a

misnomer. Those who expounded the monopsychistic theory,[1] for example, did not do so because it was the theory of Averroes but because they believed it to be the theory of Aristotle, rightly interpreted by Averroes. To call them 'Averroists', then, is to place the emphasis wrongly: they should rather be called 'integral Aristotelians'. This contention seems to me very reasonable. In the list of propositions which were condemned at Paris in 1270 and again in 1277 some affected the doctrine of Avicenna no less than that of Averroes. For example, the theory of the eternity of the world was censured. But this theory was held by Avicenna as well as by Averroes; and it was held by them, as also by the 'Averroists' of the faculty of arts at Paris, largely because it was the theory of Aristotle (with the difference that there is no doctrine of creation in Aristotle, whereas both Avicenna and Averroes maintained the ontological dependence of the world on God). The principal theory which was peculiar to Averroes's interpretation of Aristotle was human monopsychism, asserted in a form which involved the denial of personal immortality; and this theory was likewise censured at Paris; but it was by no means the only offending proposition put forward by the 'Averroists', even if it was the one which excited most attention. There is good reason, then, for calling the 'Averroists' 'integral Aristotelians', as the name 'Averroist' overemphasizes one particular theory. But, after all, the name does not matter very much; and it is more convenient to call them 'Averroists' than to speak always of 'integral Aristotelians'. The important thing, however, is to realize that it was Aristotle who

[1] See pp. 65–6.

was regarded as 'the Philosopher'. Averroes was esteemed as 'the commentator'.

When the Averroists or integral Aristotelians were attacked for their theologically unorthodox opinions and statements, they made a curious reply. They said that they were simply engaged in reporting the doctrines of Aristotle. In other words, they gave as a reason for their lack of concern about the conciliation of philosophy with theology the statement that they were acting as historians. The authors of the condemnation of 1277 asserted that some members of the faculty of arts maintained that the offending propositions were 'true according to philosophy, but not according to the Catholic faith'. If this assertion really represents the mind of the Averroists, their position might be interpreted in various ways. It might be that the Averroists were putting forward a 'double-truth' theory out of the prudent desire to avoid a charge of heresy. It might even be that there was the concealed implication that the Christian revelation is a fable. If, however, the explanation of their position which was attributed to them was seriously intended it would have to be interpreted as meaning, for example, that the human intellect, which in the natural order (with which philosophy is concerned) would be numerically one and the same in all members of the species, has been miraculously multiplied by the divine activity, with which theology is concerned. The trouble is, however, that this is not what the Averroists actually said. Siger of Brabant, for instance, said quite explicitly that there is only one truth, namely the revealed truth, and that the object of philosophy is simply to report and interpret the opinions of the philosophers, above all that of Aristotle. This being the purpose of philosophy, the opinions of Aristotle must be faithfully reported, even if they conflict with what we know to be true. If this represents the real mind of the Averroists, it would appear that when the authors of the condemnation of 1277 attributed the double-truth theory to the Averroists they were stating what they took to be the logical consequences of their position. It would also follow that a man like Siger of Brabant reduced the function of the philosopher to that of the historian of philosophy. In this case there would be all the more reason for saying that it is useless to look to the thirteenth-century Averroists for constructive philosophic thought; for they would be engaged, according to their own claim, simply in reporting the opinions of past philosophers. If, however, we suppose that the authors of the condemnation spoke with a greater knowledge of the real mind of the Averroists than we can possess, it would follow that their reply was not sincere. The evidence is really insufficient to enable us to decide conclusively whether the reply of the Averroists was sincere or not, or, if it was insincere, precisely what their real mind was. It is, however, significant that St. Thomas evidently did not consider that the Averroists were really engaged in a mere reporting of Aristotle's ideas. It is also significant that after the condemnation of 1270 the Averroists, or some of them, continued to teach in secret what they had previously taught in public.

Siger of Brabant (c. 1235–82), who taught in the faculty of arts at Paris, was the best-known member of the group. He professed, as we have seen, to expound the philosophy of Aristotle. The world was represented, in this exposition, as eternal: and no species had any first member. There is a recurrent cyclic process of determined events; and God exercises no providence. In man the intellect is a separate principle, numerically one in all men, the activity of which is conditioned by the different images caused by the different sense-experiences. There is no personal immortality.

It has been maintained that after the condemnation of 1270 Siger of Brabant modified his opinions in the direction of Thomism. The evidence is not very clear on this point. But in any case, if one were to take Siger's assertion at its face value, namely that he had been merely reporting the opinions of Aristotle and not asserting his own beliefs, his retractations would be rather changes in his interpretation of Aristotle than in his own opinions. But it may be that the retractations indicated a real change of opinion.

In 1277 a further condemnation took place, some 219 propositions being censured by Étienne Tempier, bishop of Paris. The condemnation was levelled chiefly against Siger of Brabant and Boethius of Dacia, a Swede. Among other things the latter maintained that philosophers alone can attain true happiness, which consists in the knowledge of truth and the practice of the good, that is, in the natural development of man's highest faculties. It is quite clear that Boethius was expounding the idea of happiness which is to be found in the *Ethics* of Aristotle. But was he merely reporting Aristotle, or was he giving his own opinion, in abstraction from all theological considerations and without meaning to deny the Christian doctrine that man's final end. which is

by no means confined to philosophers, is a supernatural beatitude, attainable in the next life? We do
not really know the answer to this question.

But, though the condemnation of 1277 was
directed principally against Siger and Boethius, it
affected, and was meant to affect, some propositions
held by Aquinas and certain other theologians. It
would appear that the intention was to associate the
Christian Aristotelianism of Aquinas with the hetero-
dox Aristotelianism expounded in the faculty of arts,
and so to compass the ruin of both. Possibly the
hostility of the secular clergy against the regular
clergy played some part in the affair. In any case
St. Thomas had already made it quite clear that he
was no Averroist. He composed his work *On the
Unity of the Intellect against the Averroists* in 1270,
the year of the first condemnation. But certain
of his doctrines (for example, the theory of matter
as the principle of individuation) which were affected
by the condemnation of 1277 were held also by Siger
of Brabant. This was only natural, since they came
from Aristotle or were developments of Aristotelian
doctrines. There can be little doubt, then, that those
who drew up the list of propositions condemned in
1277 were hostile to Aristotelianism in general. But
if they intended to give Aristotelianism its death-
blow, they did not meet with the success for which
they hoped. It was too late to return to the position
which obtained before the newly-introduced works of
Aristotle had impressed the best minds among the
theologian-philosophers by their scope and pro-
fundity and captured the enthusiasm of the professors
of the faculty of arts who were no longer content with
the tasks hitherto assigned them.

CHAPTER VIII

DUNS SCOTUS

1. WHEN we think of British philosophers, we tend to think of Hobbes, Locke, Berkeley, Hume, Mill, and other lights of modern philosophy. Possibly the name of Roger Bacon may occur to the mind as well as that of Francis Bacon; but few people would think of Duns Scotus. Yet he was one of the most able and acute philosophers whom Britain has produced. Of a critical turn of mind, and gifted with an ability to discover fine distinctions and shades of meaning (an ability which won for him his traditional title of 'the subtle Doctor'), he possessed at the same time a remarkable power of constructive systematization. As a Franciscan, he was naturally influenced by the philosophic traditions of his Order; yet he was also strongly influenced by Aristotelianism and by Islamic philosophy, particularly, perhaps, by the thought of Avicenna. But he brought to bear on the various elements which helped to form his philosophy the power of an original, constructive, and critical mind.

Born in Scotland about the year 1265 John Duns Scotus entered the Franciscan Order in 1278. He subsequently lectured both at Oxford and Paris; and his lectures in these two centres are represented by the two sets of commentaries on the *Sentences* of Peter Lombard, the *Opus Oxoniense* and the *Reportata Parisiensia*. These works embody additions made by disciples, while of the other works formerly attributed to Scotus some are now definitely rejected as unauthentic. Until very recently there was no critical edition of Scotus's writings; but in 1950 the Franciscan Fathers published at Rome the first two volumes of the long awaited critical edition of the *Opera Omnia.* The completion of this great work will make it possible to form a really accurate and reliable picture of the actual teaching of Scotus in its development. Meanwhile, however, any account of his system must necessarily be to a certain extent provisional. In any case all that I can attempt in this chapter is to give an outline of some aspects of his thought.

2. Let us take first of all an aspect of Scotus's thought which appears to me at least to be characteristic. His whole philosophy rests on the conviction that the human mind is able to apprehend being and objective truth. Aquinas, of course, obviously possessed the same conviction. But Scotus considered that the objectivity of human knowledge involves certain positions which were not allowed for, or which were not sufficiently admitted, by a philosopher like Aquinas. I want to illustrate this point by some examples of Scotus's line of thought.

Scotus was at one with Aquinas in saying that human knowledge depends on experience. He discarded the traditional Augustinian-Franciscan theory of a special divine illumination and held, with Aquinas, that the Aristotelian doctrine of the abstraction of the universal can explain the genesis of human knowledge without its being necessary to invoke either innate ideas or a special divine illumination. But he was not prepared to accept Aquinas's doctrine that the human mind does not know individual things directly or immediately. According to

Aquinas, the direct object of human intellectual knowledge is the form abstracted from matter, which is the principle of individuation, and known through the universal concept. The senses apprehend the individual thing; but the mind apprehends it only indirectly, as represented in the image or phantasm. There is no intellectual intuition of the individual thing as such. Scotus rejected this view in favour of the view that the mind does have a primary intellectual, though confused, intuition of the individual thing as such. How, he asks, could we abstract the universal from the individual thing without a previous intellectual intuition of the individual thing? If the mind abstracts, it abstracts from what it knows. Abstraction, then, presupposes this intuition of the individual thing; and, if there were no such intuition on the part of the mind, there would be no guarantee of the objective reference and foundation of our abstract universal ideas.

Again, Scotus's realism can be looked at from an analogous point of view. If one asserts that Socrates is a man and that Plato is a man, there must be in both Socrates and Plato a human nature which is in itself 'indifferent' to being the nature of Socrates or Plato (if, that is, the judgements are objectively true). Scotus did not mean, of course, that the human nature of Socrates is numerically the same as that of Plato, or that we can predicate of Plato the actual human nature of Socrates. What he thought was that we can distinguish in Socrates his 'Socratesness' from his human nature. This human nature, though numerically distinct from that of Plato, is not identical with the 'Socratesness' of Socrates. Of what kind. then. is the distinction between Socrates's

'Socratesness' and his human nature? It is not a
distinction between two separable things: not even
the divine power could separate the two. But neither
is it a purely mental distinction. It is a 'formal
objective distinction'. This distinction, which was
not invented by Scotus, though he made an extensive
use of it, can be illustrated perhaps by an example.
Reasoning and sensation are objectively distinct;
but the faculty of reasoning and the principle of
sensitive life in the human soul are not separable in
the way that soul and body are separable. The power
of reasoning and the power (not necessarily the
actuality) of exercising sensitive life could not be
separated without the destruction of the soul. The
distinction is one between different 'formalities'
rather than between separable things. Scotus's
realism involved the belief that there exists in each
individual thing a nature distinct from its 'thisness';
and he thought that this belief was implied in the
objective reference of our universal judgements.
But he was not an ultra-realist in the sense of attri-
buting the numerically same nature to all members
of the same species. Nevertheless, his realism seemed
excessive to William of Ockham, who attacked it
strongly.

Finally, Scotus concerned himself with the objective character of metaphysical statements about God.
Suppose that we speak of God as being, for example,
necessary being in contradistinction to contingent
being. The term 'being' is first applied to the finite
things we experience; and the mind, by reflection on
finite being, passes to the idea of divine being. We
may reason on the following lines. If contingent
being exists, necessary being exists. But contingent

being exists. Therefore necessary being exists. Now, if this syllogism is to be valid, said Scotus, there must be some sense in which the term 'being', as used of contingent being and necessary being, has the same meaning. If the meaning is not in any way the same, and if at the same time we have no intuition of God but come to a philosophical knowledge of God only through reflection on the finite beings of experience, the term 'being', as applied to God, has no meaning for us. There must, therefore, be a univocal concept of being, applicable to both God and creatures.

Perhaps the point can be made clearer if we take a term like 'wisdom'. Our idea of wisdom is formed through experience of human wisdom. But we cannot predicate human wisdom of God. On the other hand, if the term as predicated of God is used equivocally, that is, in a completely different sense, it has no meaning for us. We must, then, according to Scotus, be able to extract, as it were, from the idea of human wisdom some idea of wisdom in itself, which can be predicated univocally of human beings and of God. All our language about God, if it is significant, presupposes that the mind possesses such univocal concepts, formed through experience of finite beings but applicable also to the divine being.

Scotus did not mean to say that infinite being and finite being are actually being in the same sense. He did not think that the term 'being' is a genus. The univocal concept of being was, for him, the idea of opposition to nothingness. In actual fact, in the real order, God and creatures are opposed to nothingness in different ways; but unless the mind has a kind of minimum idea of opposition to nothingness, prescinding from the ways in which different being are opposed to nothingness, it could never, according to Scotus, pass from creatures to God. In the language of the syllogism, there would be no middle term. There are, of course, considerable objections to this theory; but, whether it is a valid theory or not, Scotus was no pantheist. He did not deny analogy: he held rather that analogy presupposes the possession of univocal concepts. We should be unable, in his view, to compare creatures with God, in respect of their being and attributes, unless there were concepts applicable to both. His contention was, then, that Thomist natural theology, at least as he interpreted it, leads to agnosticism, unless analogy is recognized as presupposing univocal concepts.

3. From what has been said it should be clear how absurd is the contention that Scotus destroyed scholastic metaphysics. On the contrary, he was concerned to improve its foundations. He was himself a metaphysician of distinction and acuteness; and his discussions of being and its attributes, of causes, of the divine infinity, are certainly not inferior to those of other medieval thinkers. In some respects, too, he was a traditionalist, though when he adopted traditional Franciscan positions he sometimes gave them a new form. For example, medieval thinkers had taken pleasure in discussing whether the intellect or the will is the nobler faculty. Aquinas came down on the side of the intellect, whereas the Augustinian-Franciscan tradition favoured the will, largely on the ground that love is better than knowledge. On this matter Scotus followed the Franciscan tradition. But, though he gave the traditional reasons for this position, he laid the chief emphasis on liberty. If the intellect apprehends truth, it cannot

restrain its assent; but the will is essentially a free power. It is difficult for us to feel much enthusiasm or excitement over the dispute about the faculties; but the point I want to make is that Scotus took the traditional dispute and made it the opportunity for a discussion of freedom and its relation to knowledge.

How, then, did the impression arise that Scotus used his critical faculty in such a way that he undermined the scholastic metaphysics and prepared the way for the more radical criticism which arose in the fourteenth century? The impression is partly derived from the *Theoremata*, which is now not generally thought to be an authentic work of Scotus. Its unauthenticity is not admitted by everyone; but until, if ever, the work is proved to be authentic, it is best to confine the discussion to the works which are recognized as authentic. In these works it is perfectly clear that Scotus criticized arguments of previous and contemporary metaphysicians; but it is also clear that his line of criticism did not amount to anything resembling a destruction of scholasticism. I want now to show this by some examples.

We have seen that Aquinas laid stress on the Aristotelian proof from motion for God's existence. Scotus clearly had no firm belief in the cogency of this proof. He questioned the validity of the principle on which it rests, namely that whatever is moved is moved by something else. In regard to spiritual beings, he said, like angels or the human soul the principle is false, while even in regard to bodies its universal validity is questionable. But this does not mean that Scotus thought it impossible to prove God's existence. One of his objections to the motion argument as such was that it keeps within the physical order and, even if valid would not prove the existence of what we understand by 'God'. To do this, we have to keep to properly metaphysical arguments. In no certainly authentic work does Scotus say that God's existence cannot be proved. On the contrary, he concentrated on metaphysical arguments; and he dwelt at great length on the proofs of God's infinity, which was a favourite theme. God was for him pre-eminently the infinite being and not an astronomical hypothesis.

It is true that Scotus did not believe that one can 'demonstrate' all those attributes of God which were generally thought to be demonstrable. In one certainly authentic work he lists a number of divine attributes which are known only by revelation. Among these is omnipotence. But here again his position was not nearly so revolutionary as might perhaps at first sight appear. That God possesses infinite power, in the sense that He can produce every possible effect either mediately (through secondary causes) or immediately can be proved by philosophers. What they cannot prove is that God can produce all possible effects immediately, for, as far as the philosopher can see, the imperfection of some effects might postulate the causal operation of a subordinate finite cause.

Another example of Scotus's criticism of traditional positions is his criticism of the philosophical arguments for immortality. A favourite Augustinian-Franciscan argument was based on the desire for perfect happiness, which was said to involve a natural desire for immortality. Scotus asks what is meant by 'natural desire'? If it means, for example, the biological urge to preserve one's life, which is shown by avoiding what experience has shown to lead to death, one might just as well argue that brute animals are immortal as that human souls are immortal. If, however, it means a conscious desire, one cannot argue from the desire for immortality to the fact of immortality, unless one has first shown that the human soul can survive bodily death. Scotus did not think that this had been demonstrated. He was not denying immortality: what he said was that the arguments for immortality are not demonstrative, though some of them, like that from the soul's intellectual activity, are highly probable. Certainty concerning immortality is attained only through revelation. Ockham, too, thought that immortality cannot be proved philosophically.

4. Scotus has often been represented as a precursor of Ockham in his doctrine of the relation of the moral law to the divine will.[1] But Scotus did not simply make the divine will the measure of good and evil, right and wrong. He explicitly states that there are unalterable moral principles, the obligatory character of which is self-evident. God could not order the opposite, not because He is subject to law, but because these principles are ultimately founded on the divine nature or essence. God could not, without violating His own nature (which is impossible) order a man to hate Him or to love other gods than Himself. This insistence on unalterable precepts of the moral law differentiates Scotus's position from that of Ockham, according to whom God could, absolutely speaking, order a man to hate Him. But

[1] Ockham maintained that the moral law depends on the divine choice, in the sense that God could have instituted a different moral order from the one He has actually instituted.

there are, according to Scotus, other precepts of the natural law which are not so necessary and self-evident that God cannot dispense from them in particular cases. Scotus was thinking of apparent cases of dispensation in the Old Testament; and in view of these cases, interpreted as real cases of dispensation, he felt himself compelled to say that the precepts of the second table of the decalogue[1] are not so necessary that God cannot dispense. In this sense their obligatory character may be said to depend on the divine will. Scotus insisted, however, at the same time that the content of these precepts is not arbitrary, and that an action which falls under the natural law is prohibited because it is wrong, and not the other way round. The so-called secondary precepts of the natural law are in close harmony with the primary precepts, but the connexion is not so necessary that the Creator cannot dispense. It seems to me to be rather difficult to reconcile Scotus's various ways of speaking about the moral law; but in any case it is clear that his distinction between precepts which do not depend and precepts which in some sense do depend on the divine will for their obligatory character was not made in order to support an authoritarian theory of ethics but rather in order to explain certain difficulties in Scriptural exegesis.

If we look back on Scotus from a position in history subsequent to the fourteenth century it is possible, of course, to see his philosophy as a precursor of Ockhamism. It is possible to say, for instance, that Scotus's repudiation of certain arguments employed by previous metaphysicians was a

[1] That is, the commandments bearing on the relations of human beings to one another.

stage on the way to Ockham's more radical and extensive criticism, and that his theory of the relation of the secondary precepts of the natural law to the divine will was a preparation for Ockham's thorough-going subordination of the moral law to the divine choice. This is a reasonable point of view, I think. But if one leaves subsequent history out of account and considers Scotus's philosophy simply in itself and in relation to Scotus's predecessors and contemporaries, rather than in relation to his successors, it clearly belongs to the great group of thirteenth-century syntheses. Scotus lived and wrote at the turn of the century, and in a sense his philosophy, in its critical aspects, looked forward to Ockhamism; but Scotus himself was a convinced metaphysician, and, even if he thought that the proofs for immortality, for example, were only probable arguments, he by no means relinquished the idea that one can prove a great number of metaphysical positions with certainty. William of Ockham was a resolute opponent of Scotus; and the Scotists have never recognized in the 'nominalists' their comrades-in-arms.

CHAPTER IX

FOURTEENTH CENTURY (1):
WILLIAM OF OCKHAM

1. THE outstanding metaphysicians and system-builders of the Middle Ages belonged to the thirteenth century. In the fourteenth century these systems lived on as bodies of doctrine characteristic of definite schools. Moreover, these schools tended to be associated with definite religious Orders. Thus, Thomism came to be characteristic of the Dominican Order, while the Franciscans, at a later date, came to regard Duns Scotus as their particular Doctor. The Hermits of St. Augustine tended to follow Giles of Rome. In the course of time these schools produced expositions of, and learned commentaries on, the works and thoughts of the thirteenth-century philosophers, the first outstanding commentator on St. Thomas being Joannes Capreolus (c. 1380–1444). Some of the later commentators, like the great Thomist, Thomas de Vio (1468–1534), commonly known as Cajetan, were much more than expositors and commentators; but in the fourteenth century these schools did not produce much creative work. Their association with definite persistent corporations like the religious Orders ensured, however, to the thirteenth-century systems a remarkable longevity.

These schools represented, in the fourteenth century, 'the ancient way' (*via antiqua*) or older tradition, in contrast with the new movement, 'the modern way' (*via moderna*), which is associated with the name of Ockham in particular. This new movement, known as the nominalist or terminist movement (the words 'terminism' and 'nominalism' were used synonymously), was characterized in part by the development of the terminist logic. This logic, though often called the 'new logic', was, of course, a development of the 'old logic'. The terminist logicians devoted great attention to analysing the function of terms in propositions, and the word 'terminism', when used to denote a certain logical development rather than as a synonym for nominalism in general, is associated principally with the theory of *suppositio*, namely with the theory of the term's function of standing for things in the proposition. Further mention of this theory will shortly be made in connexion with William of Ockham, who used the logical theory in his elimination of realist doctrines about universals. The new movement was also characterized by its analytical, critical, and sometimes empiricist approach to philosophical problems. The thinkers of the movement were more interested in the analytical treatment of particular problems than in the creation of comprehensive syntheses. Moreover, there was a strong tendency to regard as probable arguments previously regarded as demonstrative. The thorough-going criticism of traditional metaphysical arguments which was practised by William of Ockham and still more by a philosopher like Nicholas of Autrecourt has tended to give the impression that the movement was purely destructive in character; but the logical studies associated with the movement can hardly be properly characterized as 'destructive'. while certain aspects of the new movement favoured, if they did not directly cause, the growth of interest in problems of physical science which was an interesting feature of university life at Paris in the fourteenth century. It is true, however, that the new direction of thought tended to effect a separation between theology and philosophy. A great deal of traditional metaphysics were relegated to the sphere of faith; and logic and what one may call analysis tended to form the occupations of philosophers. In this sense the new movement did undermine the thirteenth-century synthesis (or syntheses, since there was no one thirteenth-century synthesis).

In the course of time the new movement came itself to be embodied in a school, the so-called nominalist school; but as far as the fourteenth century is concerned it is preferable, I think, to speak of a movement of thought rather than of a school. The movement was not confined to one place or to any particular corporation or religious Order. I have spoken of the association of the older systems with particular religious Orders; but this must not be taken to mean that the influence of the new movement did not penetrate into the religious Orders. Ockham himself was a Franciscan; and his influence was felt not only in his own, but also in other religious institutes. Moreover, if the influence of the new movement was not confined to any particular place or corporation, neither was it always uniform in character. Some philosophers were attracted by the terminist logic and concentrated particularly on logical studies, while others might be more interested in the critical analysis of philosophical ideas and arguments. Again, while some of those who criticized the traditional metaphysics adversely seem to have concerned themselves very little with the theological implications of their criticism, others regarded such criticism as effecting a welcome liberation of faith from the tyranny of rationalist metaphysics of pagan origin. In short, the new movement was complex in character and influence.

It will be easily understood that the new movement did not start abruptly but had its roots in the past. For example, what is generally known as 'Ockham's razor' or the principle of economy, namely the principle that one should not postulate the existence of a greater number of entities or factors when fewer will suffice, was not invented by Ockham himself. It had been employed, for instance, by Durandus (d. 1332), who can certainly not be called an Ockhamist, in the elimination of a number of entities postulated by the traditional Aristotelian psychology in order to explain abstraction. Again, the Ockhamists maintained that there is no problem of individuation, since there is no universal which needs to be individuated: a thing is individual by the very fact that it exists. But this had already been maintained by, for instance, the Franciscan friar Petrus Aureoli (d. 1322).

Nor was the terminist logic an invention of Ockham. Leaving out of account the Franciscan martyr, Raymond Lull (d. 1315), who can scarcely be called a terminist, but who anticipated, in a rudimentary fashion, Leibniz's dream of the *caracteristica universalis* and the *ars combinatoria*, one can draw attention to the lively interest shown by the thirteenth-century grammarians and logicians of the faculty of arts at Paris in what one may call the philosophy of

language and in the propositional function of terms.
Having been told by the theologians that they should
concern themselves with grammar and literature and
logic and not meddle with theology and metaphysics,
they came to interest themselves in the relation of
words to meaning and in the function of terms. In
fact, they tended to lay upon linguistic and logical
studies in relation to philosophy an emphasis analogous to that which today is laid upon mathematics in
relation to the physical sciences. At the beginning of
the *Summulae logicales* of Peter of Spain (d. 1277, if,
as is probable, he is to be identified with the man who
became Pope John XXI) we read that dialectic or
logic is the art of arts and the science of sciences
which prepares the way for the study of all other
sciences. Logic is the art of reasoning; but reasoning
takes place by means of language; and so the study
of logic must begin with a consideration of the word
or term and its function. This short treatise was one
of the most influential productions of the thirteenth
century; and it certainly had a profound effect on
Ockham. The principles of his logic were taken from
the manuals of thirteenth-century logicians like Peter
of Spain, though he utilized the logic of terms in
support of philosophical positions which were his
own.

There is a further point to be noticed. When the
thirteenth-century logicians exalted 'dialectic', they
often meant dialectical syllogisms leading to probable
conclusions, in contrast with demonstrative syllogisms on the one hand and sophistical syllogisms on
the other. The exaltation of dialectic tended, therefore, to express a concentration on probable reasoning. This is not to say that the logicians in question

thought that no certainty can be attained in philosophy; but it would seem that the attention which they gave to dialectical reasoning influenced the fourteenth-century nominalists, who not infrequently regarded as merely probable, conclusions which had previously been held to be certain.

2. William of Ockham was born at Ockham in Surrey, probably between the years 1280 and 1290. He entered the Franciscan Order and did his studies at Oxford. In 1324, before he had yet begun to teach as a professor, he had to appear at Avignon in order to answer charges relating to certain propositions contained in his commentary on the *Sentences* of Peter Lombard. The affair was complicated by the fact that Ockham became involved in the dispute between Pope John XXII and the Franciscan General, Michael of Cesena, concerning evangelical poverty. In 1328 Michael of Cesena fled from Avignon, taking with him Ockham and two other Franciscans. The fugitives, who drew upon themselves a sentence of excommunication, took refuge with Ludwig of Bavaria, whom they joined at Pisa and accompanied to Munich. Ockham took part in the struggle between pope and emperor by means of his politico-ecclesiastical writings; but his ideas on the relation between the two powers will be briefly considered in a later chapter. He died in 1349, probably of the Black Death. It is not known whether the steps he had taken to effect a reconciliation with the Holy See led to a successful issue before he died.

There are various elements or strands in Ockham's philosophy; and perhaps one may consider first the 'empiricist' aspect. Ockham insisted strongly on the primacy of intuition or the immediate perception of individual things. 'Nothing can be known naturally in itself unless it is known intuitively.' It is true that intuitive knowledge is not for Ockham precisely the same as perception, for intuitive knowledge in the full sense involves the judgement that the thing perceived exists; but the judgement that a thing exists is the natural result of the perception, and the truth of the judgement is guaranteed by the perception. Ockham, however, qualified this by saying that God could, for example, act on a man in such a way that he believed a star to be present to his vision when it was not there. But he did not think that the philosopher can prove that God can act in this way. In any case, in the natural course of events intuitive knowledge is self-guaranteed. This is the necessary foundation of all knowledge about the world. Knowledge about the world is based, in other words, on experience; and experience is experience of individual things. Ockham thus shows his feeling for the concrete and individual, and his conviction of the fundamental importance of experiential or intuitive knowledge.

Ockham did not show any strong personal interest in physical science; nor (it scarcely needs to be said) had he any understanding of modern scientific method. But it is clear that his insistence on the experiential foundation of knowledge about the world would naturally favour the growth of physical science, in the sense that its natural effect would be to concentrate attention on the observable facts. Moreover, his use of 'the razor' or principle of economy is closely connected with this insistence on experience. For, if it is intuition or direct experience alone which

guarantees the existence of a thing, one can profitably get rid of all alleged entities the existence of
which cannot be verified in experience, provided,
Ockham would add, that their existence is not known
through revelation.

An important conclusion was drawn by Ockham
from the foregoing considerations. That one thing is
the efficient cause of another thing can be established
only by experience. If the presence of A is followed
by the presence of B, and if, in the absence of A,
B does not follow, even when all the other conditions
are present which normally precede or accompany
the presence of B, it must be taken that A is the
efficient cause of B. In determining the cause of B
one should observe the principle of economy, eliminating all factors which empirical investigation does not
show to be constantly followed by the presence of
B. This is, of course, a method of ascertaining the
cause of a given event rather than a statement that
causality means simply regular succession. However, Ockham's contention that it cannot be demonstrated but only empirically established that one
thing is the cause of another, would seem to rule
out the causal argument in natural theology.

Secondly, there are the logical and rationalist elements in his philosophy. In the Ockhamist logic a
distinction was drawn between meaning and substi-
tution or standing-for (*suppositio*). Terms acquire
the function of standing for something only in the
proposition. In the proposition, 'this man is walking', the term, 'this man', stands for a definite
individual. But in the proposition, 'man is mortal',
the term stands for a class, while in the proposition, 'man is a masculine noun', a grammarian's

statement is made about the word 'man'. *Suppositio* is, therefore, of different kinds.

At this point one may ask what it is precisely for which the term 'man' stands in the proposition, 'man is mortal'. Does it stand for a universal reality, a universal existing outside the mind? Certainly not, answers Ockham. Only individuals exist. The term 'man', therefore, in the proposition mentioned stands for individual men. Universality belongs to terms or names, which are signs for classes of individual things.

In so far as Ockham says that universality belongs to terms or names, he may be called a 'nominalist'. But it is important to realize that he made a distinction between the written word or term, the spoken word, and the term considered according to its logical significance (the *terminus conceptus* or *intentio animae*). The word considered simply as a word, written or spoken, is a conventional sign. For example, it is a matter of linguistic convention whether one uses the word 'man' or 'homme' or 'uomo'. The term considered according to its logical meaning (the concept) is, on the contrary, a natural sign: it is the same whether we use the word 'man' or the word 'homme'. When we say that Socrates is a man and that Plato is a man, we are not predicating the word, as a word, of Socrates and Plato: we are predicating the term according to its meaning. And because Socrates and Plato resemble one another, the term has the same logical significance in both cases. When we say that man is mortal, the term 'man' stands, then, for Plato and Socrates and all other individual men, for the perception of each of them produces the same idea. Although, therefore, we can speak of

Ockham as a nominalist, we can just as well, or better, speak of him as a conceptualist. His point was that the mind and individual things are quite sufficient to explain such propositions as 'man is mortal': the razor can be employed to eliminate all alleged universal existent realities. Universality is not an attribute of things: it is a function of terms in the proposition. In Ockham's discussion of universals we see how the interest is shifted from metaphysical questions to an analysis of the propositional function of terms.

The subject of Ockham's rejection of universal realities belongs perhaps rather to a discussion of the 'empirical' aspect of his philosophy; but I find it convenient to write about it here because of its connexion with his logic. Moreover, a consideration of his idea of *suppositio* puts us in a position to understand his idea of science.

All science is concerned, he says, with propositions, for it is of propositions that truth and falsity are predicated. This may sound as though he was saying that science is concerned with ideas, in the sense that science has no connexion with reality. But this is not the case. Ockham made a distinction between 'real science' and 'rational science'. Real science is concerned directly with propositions, and so with terms; but these terms stand, as we have seen, for things. There is, therefore, no unbridgeable gulf between real science and things. Let us suppose that the proposition, 'man is mortal', is a proposition of real science. It is the proposition which is said to be true and which is the immediate object of science; but the term 'man' stands for individual men. Science is concerned, then, with reality, though indirectly. As

to rational science, this is concerned with terms which
do not stand directly for things. Terms like 'genus'
and 'species' are not 'terms of first intention' standing directly for things: they are 'terms of second intention', standing for other terms. 'Species', for
example, stands for terms like 'cow', 'horse', 'man',
which themselves stand for things: it is a class of
classes. Logic is thus a rational, and not a real,
science. It is essential to remember this, says Ockham, if one is to avoid the temptation of interpreting
logical terms as if they referred directly to entities.
Neither the Tree of Porphyry nor the Categories of
Aristotle refers to entities which actually exist; they
treat of terms or of our conceptual classifications.

Now Ockham, contrary to what one might perhaps expect, had a great respect for deductive or
syllogistic reasoning; and it is as well to bear this
in mind when one is speaking of him as an 'empiricist'.
He admitted self-evident principles, the truth of
which is evident once the terms are understood.
These propositions are not simply empirical hypo-
theses: they are, in one of the modern uses of the
word, analytic. They do not constitute 'science'; for
'science is the evident knowledge of necessary truths
obtainable by the application of premises in syllogistic reasoning'. That is to say 'science' consists of
the body of conclusions rather than the self-evident
principles on which the process of deductive reasoning is based. It is noteworthy that Ockham speaks
of 'necessary truths', obtainable by syllogistic reasoning, as constituting science. This is a thoroughly
Aristotelian view of science; and it represents the
rationalist side of Ockham's philosophy. It does not
follow that this view of science is in conflict with

Ockham's insistence on the experiential origin of factual knowledge. For example, even if the proposition that the whole is greater than the part is a necessary proposition, it is by experience that we form the ideas of whole and part. There may, indeed, be difficulties in reconciling the rationalist and empiricist elements in Ockham's philosophy; but the two elements are there none the less. The fact is that Ockham looked on himself as more genuinely Aristotelian than realists like Scotus; and he was naturally influenced both by Aristotle's profound respect for deductive reasoning, and by the 'empiricist' aspects of Aristotelianism. Ockham's criticism of previous metaphysical arguments certainly affected some undoubtedly Aristotelian positions; but it is a mistake to look on him as an anti-Aristotelian. In his view, a philosopher like Scotus was unfaithful to the true spirit of Aristotle.

Thirdly, one must take into account Ockham's criticism of arguments employed by the thirteenth-century speculative metaphysicians. In the first place, he was sceptical in regard to the demonstrative character of the traditional proofs of God's existence. Like Scotus, he questioned the principle that whatever is moved is moved by something else; and he also refused to admit the argument from finality. If one presupposes God's existence, one is entitled to speak of all things being directed to their several ends; but, if God's existence is not presupposed, all we can say is that non-intelligent agents act from a necessity of nature. As to intelligent agents, their activities can be accounted for without postulating God's existence. It is true that Ockham accepted as 'sufficient' the argument brought to show that there is a first or supreme conserver of the world here and now; but it must be added that he thought that only probable arguments can be brought to show that this being is first or supreme in an absolute sense. For he did not think that it is possible to prove strictly the unicity of the world. The existence of other worlds is conceivable, even if improbable; and so it is conceivable, even if not probable, that there is a plurality of relatively first causes or conservers. In other words, Ockham did not think that more than probable arguments can be given for the existence of an absolutely supreme, perfect, and infinite being; and he criticized adversely Scotus's arguments for the divine unicity and infinity. As to the divine attributes, he maintained that it is impossible to demonstrate those attributes like omnipotence and omniscience which are peculiar to God, on the ground that there can be no middle term in the relevant syllogisms, if our philosophical knowledge of God must be based on experience of creatures. If, however, we assume God's existence, we can indeed argue that God is good, on the ground, for example, that goodness is found in creatures and is an attribute of being. But even so all we can attain is a nominal representation of the divine reality: we are arguing about 'names' or concepts rather than about the divine reality itself. Perhaps one is not misrepresenting Ockham if one says that he regarded philosophical discussions about the divine attributes as discussions about the proper use of words.

The traditional arguments in philosophical psychology were also questioned by Ockham. As far as strict philosophic argument is concerned, it cannot be shown that the soul does not owe its existence to

natural generation; and the arguments advanced to
prove the immateriality and immortality of the soul
do not amount to demonstrations. Nor can it be
proved that man enjoys free will, although our habit
of praising and blaming people for their actions shows
that we accept the reality of freedom. We know
experientially that the will is capable of choosing or
not choosing the act proposed by the reason; but a
demonstration of freedom is not forthcoming. Ockham had a strict idea of what constitutes a demonstration, namely a necessary deduction from necessary
principles; and when he says that this or that metaphysical argument is not a demonstration, he means
just this. He does not mean, in other words, to cast
doubts on the existence of God or the immortality of
the soul. What he thought was that we know both
the existence of God in the proper sense, that is,
as infinite, omnipotent, omniscient and absolutely
supreme and perfect being, and the immortality of
the soul only by faith. For Ockham was not a modern
sceptic or 'rationalist': he was a Franciscan and a
theologian as well as a philosopher.

Finally, then, one must take into account the
theological element in Ockham's thought. He considered that the divine omnipotence and freedom are
known only by faith, by the acceptance of revealed
truth; but his extremely strong convictions on the
subject of the divine omnipotence had an important
influence on his philosophy. It is not always easy to
assess how much he was influenced by logical considerations and by his 'empiricism' in asserting a
given opinion and how much by theological considerations; but the latter cannot be passed over
as unimportant. For example, he rejected the

traditional Augustinian doctrine of the divine ideas.
He was willing to use the language of the doctrine
to a certain extent; but the divine ideas were for him
not universal archetypes but individual creatures as
known by God. And to use the phrase 'divine idea'
in this sense was tantamount to a rejection of the
traditional doctrine. Now, it is clear that Ockham's
empiricism and his dislike of all realism in the matter
of universals predisposed him to adopt the position
which he did adopt in regard to the divine ideas. But
there was another consideration which weighed with
him. In his view, the introduction of Greek metaphysics into Christian theology had made the theologians talk as though God, in His creative activity,
were guided or ruled by ideas or patterns of creation.
But to say this is, in Ockham's opinion, to limit or
circumscribe the divine freedom and omnipotence.
In other words, he considered that the Greek metaphysics of the thirteenth-century theologian-philosophers had contaminated the purity of the Christian
faith. To get rid of this metaphysic is to liberate
Christian theology from an alien yoke. Of course, if
the traditional metaphysics were ousted, the natural
result would be that theology and philosophy would
tend to fall apart; and this is what happened in Ockham's case. But it is a mistake to think that he
separated philosophy from theology simply out of a
desire to purify philosophy from theological influences. He wanted also to purify theology from
what he regarded as the contamination of pagan metaphysics. And if we wish to understand the mind of the
historic Ockham and to avoid turning him into a
modern rationalist, it is important to realize this
point.

But it is in his ethics that Ockham's theological pre-
occupations are shown most closely. Freedom is the
special mark of personality; and the infinite divine
freedom is shown in the divine omnipotence. In man,
however, the will is subject to moral obligation,
whereas God cannot be subject to obligation. It is
the divine will which imposes the moral law which
man is obliged to obey. 'By the very fact that God
wills something, it is right for it to be done.' Ockham does, indeed, give a traditional view of morality
when he says that 'nothing is dear to God unless it is
good'; but he insists that it is good because God wills
it. And he was quite prepared to draw the logical
consequences from this position. Adultery, for example, is wrong; but it is wrong because God has forbidden it. If God were to order adultery, it would be
meritorious. Absolutely speaking, God could even
command a man to hate Him.

Ockham did not mean to imply, of course, that in
the present moral order adultery or murder or hatred
of God can be right. His position was rather that the
present moral order depends on God's choice. God
could, absolutely speaking, have imposed a different
moral law; but in point of fact He has imposed the
one which actually obtains. Ockham was not concerned with weakening moral obligation or with pro-
moting disbelief in the moral law; he was concerned
with exalting the divine freedom and omnipotence
and drawing what he considered to be the logical
consequences of the divine omnipotence. One of the
great difficulties about a purely authoritarian moral
theory, however, is that we could hardly know what
God has ordered except through divine revelation.
Ockham speaks sometimes of the rule of morality as

'right reason'; and he admits that one is always bound
to follow one's conscience, even if it is erroneous.
'A created will which follows an invariably erroneous
conscience is a right will.' But unless Ockham meant
that the function of right reason is simply that of per-
ceiving that God's commands are to be obeyed, it is
rather difficult to see what moral function it could
exercise if moral precepts depend on God's arbitrary
choice.

It is clear, then, that Ockham, as a theologian or as
a philosopher accepting propositions known only by
faith, emphasized the divine omnipotence on the one
hand and the dependence of individual finite things
on the other. We could never really demonstrate the
existence of A from the existence of B, because, if A
and B are distinct, God could cause one to exist without the other. This position has immediate reper-
cussions in regard to 'science'. Ockham, as we have
seen, admitted 'real' science as distinct from
'rational' science; but, once given his rejection of the
metaphysic of essences, real science, considered as
demonstrative, can scarcely be more than a demonstration of the implications of terms, premises, and
definitions: it keeps within the purely conceptual
sphere. The conclusion of a syllogism in real science
may be verified empirically: but, if so, it happens to
be verified empirically. There is no absolute necessity
for its being empirically verified, since nothing in the
world is necessary. Ockham would claim, of course,
that this was the true Christian view of the matter;
and that the idea of necessary causal connexions had
been imported from pagan philosophy to the detri-
ment of Christian thought.

It is fairly obvious that if one translates Ockham's

philosophy into modern terms he can be made to appear highly up-to-date. The rationalist side of his philosophy can be represented by the thesis that logical and analytic propositions and implications are certain but give no factual information about the world, while the empirical side of his philosophy can be represented by the thesis that factual propositions capable of empirical verification are never absolutely certain or necessary. There is, I think, a great deal of truth in this picture; but it is very far from being the whole. As we have seen, Ockham was a theologian, deeply convinced of the divine freedom and omnipotence; and his philosophical positions were partly determined by his theological convictions. His philosophy is complex, just as he himself was a complex personality; and its character must be seen in the light of its medieval setting, if it is to be understood.

CHAPTER X

FOURTEENTH CENTURY (2): THE OCKHAMIST MOVEMENT

1. THE influence of the 'modern' current of thought associated with the name of William of Ockham extended far and wide in the fourteenth century. We find, for example, the Franciscans Adam Wodham or Goddam (d. 1358) and John of Rodington (d. 1348), who both taught at Oxford, questioning the philosophic proofs of God's existence, unicity and omnipotence, while the Dominican Robert Holkot (d. 1349), who taught theology at Cambridge, maintained that only analytic propositions are certain (with the consequence that the proposition that God exists is not philosophically certain) and that the categories are words or concepts, not objective modes of being. Holkot, however, being a theologian, was not a religious sceptic or agnostic; and he postulated a 'logic of faith', distinct from the natural logic of Aristotle. Richard Swineshead and William Heytesbury, both of Merton College, Oxford, developed the terminist logic. Gregory of Rimini, who became General of the Hermits of St. Augustine and died in 1358, was influenced on certain points by Ockham, while Thomas Bradwardine, who taught at Oxford and died as archbishop of Canterbury in 1349, was at one with Ockham in emphasizing the divine liberty and omnipotence and in maintaining the dependence of the moral law on the divine will. A statute was enacted in 1389 at the university of Vienna, requiring

136

students in the faculty of arts to attend lectures on
the logical works of Peter of Spain, while later statutes
imposed a similar obligation in regard to the logical
writings of Heytesbury and other Ockhamist writers.
Ockhamism was also strongly represented in the universities of Heidelberg (founded in 1386), Erfurt
(1392), Leipzig (1409) and Cracow (1397). Indeed,
the university of Leipzig is said to have owed its
origin to the exodus of Ockhamists from Prague,
where John Hus and Jerome of Prague taught the
Scotist realism which they learnt from John Wycliffe
(*c.* 1320–84). Thus, in the fifteenth century, the influence of Ockhamism was strong at Paris and
Oxford and in the German universities, though at
Cologne (1389) the doctrines of St. Albert the Great
and St. Thomas Aquinas held the field, in spite of
efforts made to induce the university authorities to
discard realism in favour of nominalism. These
efforts were made because it was thought in some
quarters that the heresies of John Hus followed
from his philosophic realism; but the university
of Cologne replied that this was untrue. Louvain,
founded in 1425, was also a stronghold of the older
tradition.

Two interesting thinkers associated with the Ockhamist movement in the fourteenth century were
John of Mirecourt and Nicholas of Autrecourt. The
former, who seems to have been a Cistercian, lectured
on the *Sentences* of Peter Lombard at the Cistercian
College of St. Bernard at Paris, some of his propositions being censured by the faculty of theology in
1347. Nicholas of Autrecourt also got into trouble;
and in the same year he was expelled from the teaching body of the university of Paris. However, that

did not prevent his becoming an official of the cathedral of Metz in 1350.

2. John of Mirecourt admitted that there are some propositions which are reducible to the primary self-evident principle, the principle of contradiction. These propositions are thus analytic, in the sense that they are reducible by analysis to the principle of contradiction; and they are absolutely certain. Their truth is evident in the highest degree. Empirical propositions, however, are not of this kind, with one exception. The exception is the proposition asserting the existence of the thinker or speaker. If I say that I deny or even doubt my own existence, I am contradicting myself; for I cannot deny or even doubt my existence without implicitly affirming my existence. With this exception, however, empirical propositions are not reducible to the principle of contradiction. The principle of causality, unless it is so stated that it is a tautology, cannot be shown to depend upon the principle of contradiction in such a way that the denial of the principle of causality involves the denial of the principle of contradiction.

Critics evidently understood John as meaning that all empirical propositions are doubtful. He explains that he does not mean to deny that there are empirical propositions which are evidently true, but only that their truth is not evident to us in the same way that the truth of analytic propositions is evident. The latter possess the supreme degree of evidence (*evidentia potissima*), whereas empirical propositions cannot possess more than 'natural evidence'. The truth of some empirical propositions is doubtful, as everyone would admit; but there are other empirical propositions (for example, that there are such things as stones), the truth of which is 'naturally evident'. It is not altogether easy to see what John meant precisely by 'natural evidence', since he tends to explain away in his apologies what he had said in his commentary on the *Sentences*; but he appears to mean that, though we cannot help assenting to the truth of some empirical propositions and though it would be foolish to doubt their truth, denial of them involves no contradiction or impossibility. God, for example, could cause the appearance of a thing when the thing was not really there. As regards the principle of causality, John's position appears to be that we cannot help accepting it as a guiding principle and acting on the assumption of its truth; but its opposite is conceivable. It would follow that any proof of God's existence based on this principle could not be absolutely certain. In his first apology John asserts that the opposite of the proposition 'God exists' involves a contradiction; yet he goes on to say that a proposition of this kind does not enjoy the evidence possessed by the principle of contradiction. As these two statements appear to be incompatible, I take it that what he means is that the proposition that God exists is in itself a necessary proposition, in the sense that it is objectively impossible for God not to exist, but that no philosophical *a posteriori* proof of God's existence can be absolutely certain. Whether this is a satisfactory position or not is, of course, another question.

If the influence of Ockham is clear in the use John makes of the distinction between analytic and empirical propositions, it is clear also in the emphasis he lays on the divine freedom and omnipotence. According to him, God could, absolutely speaking, cause any act in the human will, even hatred of Himself. Again, to hate one's neighbour is sinful only because it has been prohibited by God. Naturally enough, propositions of this sort were not welcomed by the theologians; and John tried to defend himself by having it both ways. He did not mean, he explains, that hatred of one's neighbour is not contrary to the natural law; but the man who does hate his neighbour incurs or runs a risk of incurring divine punishment only because God has forbidden such hatred. Again, God cannot cause sin in the human will in such a way that He would Himself act sinfully; but, if He did cause an act of hatred of Himself in the human will, He would not sin. Distinctions of this sort clearly leave intact the idea of the moral law's dependence on the divine will. In addition, John appears to have taught a theological determinism which may betray the influence of Thomas Bradwardine's *De causa Dei*. God causes a natural deformity like blindness by not supplying the power of vision; and He causes moral deformity by not supplying moral rectitude. He admits that the Doctors do not approve of saying that God is the cause of sin, on the ground that it would follow that God sins; but he insists that God can cause sin without Himself sinning. Sin can be realized only in and through a human will; and the human will, as the 'effective' cause of the sin, acts sinfully. God cannot act sinfully; but He is none the less the 'efficacious' cause of sin, in that He wills efficaciously that there should be no moral rectitude in the will.

This authoritarian idea of the moral law, which in John of Mirecourt is coupled with theological determinism, shows how different the setting and colouring of fourteenth-century Ockhamism were from the setting and colouring of modern empiricism. Like Ockham himself, John of Mirecourt possessed a theological background; and this theological background influences his philosophy. Indeed, one can say, perhaps, that the notion of the early theologian, St. Peter Damian, that God stands, as it were, above the principles of logic and human thought was taken up again by the Ockhamists. John of Mirecourt inclined, for example, to Peter Damian's view that God could bring it about that what has actually happened in the past should not have happened in the past, while Robert Holkot, who, as already mentioned, distinguished the logic of faith from the natural logic of Aristotle, pointed to the doctrine of the Trinity as an example of a truth which transcends the Aristotelian principle of contradiction. When Holkot asserted that no philosophical theology can be called 'science', he was speaking in what he regarded as the interest of Christian faith and of dogmatic theology.

3. At the same time we notice the prominence given to the idea of analytic propositions as the only absolutely certain propositions, apart from the propositions of revealed theology. With Nicholas of Autrecourt, as with John of Mirecourt, this takes the form of insisting on the principle of contradiction as the basis of certainty. The first principle of thought, according to Nicholas, is the principle that contradictories cannot be true at the same time. This principle is first both in the negative sense that there is no prior law of thought and in the positive sense that it is presupposed by every other law of thought. Every conclusion, then, the truth of which has been demonstrated owes its certainty and evidence to the

principle of contradiction, or rather of non-contradiction. There are no degrees of certainty. A proposition (for example, the conclusion of a long chain of syllogistic reasoning) is either reducible to the first principle or it is not reducible. If it is reducible, it is certain; if it is not reducible, it is not certain. It is to be noted that Nicholas applied this doctrine to show the certainty not only of abstract propositions like 'the whole is greater than the part' but also of immediate awareness of existent data of cognition. If I see redness, for example, it is a contradiction to say that I do not see redness, for it is a contradiction to say that a colour both appears and does not appear. In other words, Nicholas admitted infallible empirical statements; and he tried to justify their certainty in a manner analogous to that in which he justified the certainty of 'analytic' statements.

One of the most interesting features of Nicholas's philosophy is his critique of causality and substance in the light of the above principle. One cannot argue with certainty from the existence of one thing to the existence of another thing. For example, the conclusion of the following argument is not certain: 'fire is applied to tow, and there is no hindrance; therefore there will be heat'. Why not? Because the propositions 'fire is applied to tow and there is no hindrance' and 'there will not be heat' are not contradictory propositions. The conclusion of the argument cannot, therefore, be reduced to the first principle; and in this case it is not certain. If we observe B constantly following A, it is probable that on any future occasion that we observe A we shall find A's occurrence followed by the occurrence of B; but it is not certain that this will happen. Nicholas takes as an example the putting of one's hand near the fire. If, he says, it has been evident to me on several occasions in the past that this action is followed by my hand's becoming warm, it is probable that my hand would become warm, if I were to put my hand near the fire now. It appears, then, that Nicholas would not allow that one can detect any necessary causal relation and that he explained our expectation of B following A in the future as due to past experience of regular sequence.

In regard to the notion of substance Nicholas maintained that we have no intuitive knowledge of material substance. As far as perception is concerned, there is no evidence that there is anything else in material things than what we actually perceive; and what we actually perceive are phenomena, not substance. On the other hand we cannot legitimately argue to the existence of unperceived substances, because we cannot argue with certainty from the existence of one thing to the existence of another thing which is not perceived. There is no contradiction involved in affirming the existence of what is perceived and denying the existence of another thing which is unperceived. Of course, if one says, 'there is an accident, therefore there is a substance', the reasoning is valid; but it is valid because an accident is defined in relation to a substance. The reasoning concerns terms or ideas, not things; for the whole question is whether one can know with certainty that what one perceives *is* an accident. One is not entitled to assume this *a priori*. In other words, *if* a perceived colour is an accident, then it inheres in a substance; but no logical contradiction is involved in affirming the appearance of the colour and yet affirming that it is not an accident inhering in a substance.

There has been some controversy as to whether Nicholas extended his critique of substance to include the soul, a spiritual substance. He asserted, indeed, that the argument, 'there is an act of understanding (or of willing); therefore there is an intellect (or a will)', is not a certain argument; but some writers have maintained that he was attacking the faculty psychology, as he remarks elsewhere that Aristotle had no certain knowledge of any substance other than his own soul. But Nicholas does not seem to be concerned to attack the doctrine of really distinct faculties, which had already been rejected by, for example, William of Ockham; and it may be possible to explain away the exception which Nicholas apparently makes in favour of knowledge of the soul's existence. Dr. Weinberg takes this line in his book on Nicholas of Autrecourt. Still, it is difficult to reach a definite conclusion in this matter.

It is not without reason, then, that Nicholas has been called the medieval Hume. But it is important to realize that he did not teach dogmatic phenomenalism. If one cannot argue with certainty from the existence of A to the existence of B neither can one argue with certainty to the non-existence of B. Nicholas maintained, for example, that we have no certain intuitive or ratiocinative knowledge of the existence of material substances; but he did not say that there are no such things as material substances. He was speaking of our knowledge rather than making affirmations about what does or does not exist.

Nicholas's critical turn of mind did not prevent his

proposing a positive philosophy of his own; but he put it forward as being no more than probable. Thus he proposed as probable the theory that the universe is perfect and eternal and that all material things are composed of atoms. Some of his conclusions were incompatible with orthodox theology; and Nicholas defended himself by observing that he only proposed his theories as probable and that it might be that someone else would show that they were not even probable. His defence was not considered satisfactory by the theologians; but we really do not know what Nicholas's subjective attitude was in regard to the relation of his theories to orthodox theology. Our main interest in Nicholas is in the use he made of his logical and epistemological principles in questioning the certainty of some of the fundamental theses of thirteenth-century metaphysics. The line he takes is quite sufficient to show that Hume was not the first philosopher to question these theses; for they had been already questioned in the fourteenth century.

4. I have said that the philosophy of William of Ockham favoured the growth of empirical science by insisting on experience as the basis of our knowledge of existent things. A statement like this needs, however, qualification. After all it would be a very naïve description either of Renaissance or of later science if one said that the scientists were men who gave more attention to factual observation than their fellows. Scientific method certainly cannot be summarized simply in terms of what Ockham would call 'intuitive knowledge'. All the same Ockhamism predisposed the minds of those who were interested in problems of physical science and of mechanics to take up these problems anew and not to be satisfied with

the solutions given, for example, by Aristotle.[1] And in point of fact we find a number of scientific problems being handled in a fresh way during the course of the fourteenth century by a group of men who were associated to some degree with the new philosophical movement. I say 'to some degree', for a man like John Buridan did not accept the more radical positions of Ockham and his successors, though he helped to develop the new logic.

The scientific movement of the fourteenth century was associated, though not exclusively, with the university of Paris. As important figures one may mention John Buridan, who was for a time rector of the university and died about 1360; Nicholas of Oresme, who taught in Paris and died as bishop of Lisieux in 1382; Albert of Saxony, who was rector of the university of Paris in 1357 and, after being the first rector of the university of Vienna in 1365, was made bishop of Halberstadt, and died in 1390; and Marsilius of Inghen, who, after having twice been rector of the university of Paris, became the first rector of Heidelberg in 1386 and died in 1396. As has been already noted, the extent to which these men can accurately be called 'Ockhamists' varies. For example, Marsilius of Inghen considered that God's existence and unicity can be proved by metaphysical arguments.

One of the physical problems to which this group of thinkers gave their attention was the problem of motion. Aristotle had made a distinction between natural and violent motion. Fire, for example, has a

---

[1] That the development of science in the fourteenth century had its roots in the scientific work of the preceding century has been noted earlier (pp. 81–3). But this fact does not exclude the influence of Ockhamism on the development of science.

natural tendency to upward motion: it is naturally light and it has a natural tendency towards its natural place. A stone on the other hand is naturally heavy and has a natural tendency towards downward motion. But if someone throws a stone upwards it moves for a time with an unnatural or violent motion, until its natural tendency to regain its natural place reasserts itself. What is the explanation of this unnatural movement? It cannot be due to the stone itself, because the stone's natural tendency is to move downwards to the earth. Nor can it be due simply to the person who throws the stone, for he is no longer in contact with the stone once it has left his hand. According to Aristotle, the man who throws the stone also moves the surrounding air, and this air moves the air farther on, each portion of the air moves the stone with it, until the successive movements of portions of air become so weak that the natural movement of the stone reasserts itself, and the stone starts to move towards its natural place.

William of Ockham had rejected this explanation of 'violent motion'. If two archers shoot at one another and the arrows meet in flight, it would be necessary to say that the same air moves in opposite directions, which is absurd. It is quite sufficient to say that a moving body moves simply because it is in motion. Possibly those are right who see in this view an anticipation of the laws of inertia; but the Paris Ockhamists preferred to have recourse to Philoponus's theory of impetus. According to this view, the moving agent impresses on the projectile a certain quality or energy, which they called 'impetus', in virtue of which the projectile continues to move after it has left the hand of the thrower, until the

impetus is overcome by the resistance of the air and
the natural weight of the body.

There are two points to notice. In the first place,
the Ockhamists gave this theory of impetus an interesting application. John Buridan maintained that
if we conceive of God as impressing a certain impetus
on the heavenly bodies at creation no further explanation of their movement is required, since they
encounter no resistance. There is no need to suppose
that they are composed of a peculiar element of their
own, and there is no need to postulate the existence
of intelligences or angels which move them. In other
words the explanation of the movements of the
celestial bodies is fundamentally the same as the
explanation of movements on the earth. Buridan
put this theory forward tentatively, saying that he
would like to know what the theologians have to say
about it; but the theory had a considerable success,
being adopted by men like Nicholas of Oresme,
Albert of Saxony, and Marsilius of Inghen. The
theory is of interest because it paves the way for a
mechanical view of the world, in which the world is
conceived as a system of bodies in motion, motion
or energy being transmitted from one body to
another.

In the second place, however, it is worth noting
that the minds of the Paris Ockhamists moved to a
great extent within the framework of the traditional
Aristotelian terms and ideas. For example, Albert
of Saxony, after raising the question whether impetus
is a substance or an accident, declared that it belongs
to the metaphysician to answer this question. He
himself asserted that it is a quality, that is to say,
an accident. Marsilius of Inghen also discussed the

question to which category or *praedicamentum* impetus should be assigned, though he gives no very definite answer.

Albert of Saxony made a distinction between the centre of gravity in a body and the centre of its volume. These two do not necessarily coincide; and it is the earth's centre of gravity, not the centre of its volume, which is really the centre of the world, in the sense that each body possessing weight tends to unite its centre of gravity with the centre of the world. This tendency is, in effect, what is meant by gravity.

One of the most remarkable figures of the group was Nicholas of Oresme. He discovered, for example, that the distance travelled by a body moving with a uniformly increasing velocity is equal to the distance travelled in the same time by a body moving with a uniform velocity equal to the velocity attained by the first body in the middle instant of its course. Moreover, in order to express these and similar successive variations of intensity in a manner which would facilitate understanding and comparison, Nicholas conceived the idea of representing them by rectangular co-ordinates, that is to say, by means of graphs. He represented space or time by a straight base line; and then he erected vertical lines on this base, the length of these vertical lines corresponding to the position or the intensity of the variable. By connecting the ends of the verticals he was thus able to obtain a curve representing the fluctuations in intensity. But, though this method prepared the way for further mathematical developments, it would be an exaggeration to depict Nicholas of Oresme as the inventor of 'analytic geometry', for the further step remained to be taken of substituting numerical equivalents for his geometrical presentation.

In his book, *Du ciel et du monde*, Nicholas of Oresme discussed the subject of the earth's movement in relation to the sun; and he proposed several reasons to show that the Ptolemaic hypothesis was by no means certain. For example, it is not possible to show by observation that the heaven rotates daily, while the earth remains stationary; for the sun would appear to move even if it was really the earth which moved and not the sun. As for objections drawn from Scriptures against the hypothesis of the earth's movement, the Scriptures speak according to the common mode of speech and should not be regarded as scientific treatises. From the statement that the sun was stayed in its course at the prayers of Joshua one is no more entitled to draw the scientific conclusion that it is the sun, and not the earth, which moves than one is entitled to draw from phrases like 'God repented' the conclusion that God can change His mind like a human being. Nicholas himself draws attention to the fact that Heraclides of Pontus had proposed the hypothesis of the earth's movement; and it appears that the contention that experience cannot prove the stationary character of the earth was already well known in the fourteenth century. But, though Nicholas maintained in his book that neither experience nor abstract reasoning can prove that the heaven rotates daily while the earth remains at rest, the conclusion at which he finally arrived was that it is the heaven, and not the earth, which moves, 'notwithstanding the reasons to the contrary, for they are persuasions which are not evidently conclusive'.

The scientific studies of the Paris Ockhamists certainly helped to prepare the way for Renaissance
science; and continuity can be traced between those
studies, for example, in mechanics, and the scientific
developments of a later period. But one should
preserve a position of moderation; and, while it is no
longer possible to represent Renaissance science as a
complete novelty, it is an exaggeration if one depicts
a man like Nicholas of Oresme as having anticipated
in the fourteenth century all the work of a Galileo.
Again, while it is true that the fresh handling of
scientific problems in the fourteenth century had
some connexion with Ockhamism, the connexion is
not so close that one can with confidence ascribe the
development of science in the fourteenth century
simply to the influence of Ockhamism. It is one
thing to say that Ockhamism, in one of its aspects,
favoured the growth of empirical science; it is another
thing to assert that Ockhamism was the sufficient
cause of that growth. An interest in scientific
matters was not exclusively a phenomenon of the
fourteenth century, though it was previously associated with Oxford rather than with Paris. What one
can, however, say is that the opening up of fresh
lines of thought in philosophy during the fourteenth
century was naturally accompanied by the opening
up of fresh lines of thought in science. No adequate
account of scientific method could possibly be given
at this period, for reflection on scientific method
follows rather than precedes concrete scientific
achievement. Moreover, the fourteenth-century
'scientists' were for the most part also philosophers;
and empirical science was not clearly distinguished
from philosophy—nor was it so distinguished for a

very considerable period. Hence it was only natural that the new philosophical movement with its criticism of preceding positions should be accompanied by a new scientific movement, also marked by criticism of preceding positions. In this sense the new scientific movement may perhaps be attributed to Ockhamism. But if one looks at the Renaissance scientists, one will see that even metaphysical philosophers can act as a kind of fertilizer for scientific development.

CHAPTER XI

SPECULATIVE MYSTICISM:
NICHOLAS OF CUSA

1. THERE had been mystics throughout the Middle Ages, of course; and as for mystical theology we have only to think of Hugh and Richard of St. Victor in the twelfth and of St. Bonaventure in the thirteenth century. In the fourteenth century, however, there was a current of philosophic speculation which was clearly influenced by reflection on mystical experience. Two themes especially stand out, the relation of finite being in general to God and the relation of the human soul in particular to God.

It is tempting perhaps to see in the flowering of speculative mysticism in the fourteenth century a reaction against the disputes and wrangling of the schools. What was more natural than that the religious consciousness should turn in disgust from the arid and inconclusive discussions of Thomists, Scotists, and Ockhamists to a line of thought which emphasized the 'one thing needful'? Some people undoubtedly did feel in this way. 'What do genera and species matter to us?' asks Thomas-à-Kempis (1380–1471). And again: 'A humble rustic who serves God is certainly better than a proud philosopher who, neglecting himself, considers the movement of the heaven.' Or, 'I desire to feel compunction rather than to know its definition.' Thomas-à-Kempis, it is true, was no philosopher; but John Gerson, who became chancellor of the university of Paris in 1395, talks in somewhat the same strain in his lectures 'against vain curiosity in the matter of faith', where he emphasizes the part played in scholastic disputes by the spirit of contention and envy, of pride and vanity and contempt for the uneducated. He insisted on the primacy of mystical theology, by which he understood the experimental knowledge of God, and he was convinced that the real remedy for the evils of his time lay in a deepening of the religious life and spirit. But he was no foe to scholastic theology and philosophy as such. Indeed, although he made extensive use of the writings of the Pseudo-Dionysius and St. Bonaventure, he was also strongly influenced by Ockhamism. The realists, he thought, confused logic with metaphysics and metaphysics with theology; they tried to understand what cannot be understood, and in the process they limited the divine freedom. Realism leads in the end to heresy. Were not John Hus and Jerome of Prague both realists?

The example of John Gerson does lend some colour to the view that speculative mysticism was a reaction against the wrangling of the schools; but it certainly does not give it unqualified support. After all, Gerson was himself theologian and philosopher. And when we turn to Meister Eckhart (c. 1260–1327), the famous German Dominican, we find a mind steeped in traditional philosophy and using the categories of traditional philosophy to express the implications of mystical experience. The speculative mystics like Eckhart focused their attention on themes which had always been present in medieval thought; and they are characterized by this focusing of attention, not by any opposition to scholasticism as such. There was, indeed, a contemporary movement for the deepening of the religious life; and this movement is borne witness to in the German sermons of Eckhart himself, of Bl. Henry Suso (d. 1366), and John Tauler (d. 1361), both Dominicans, and in the writings of the Flemish mystic, John Ruysbroeck (1293–1381). But though this movement is relevant to the focusing of attention on certain themes, this does not mean that a man like Eckhart stood apart from medieval theology and philosophy in general. The fact that Eckhart asserted propositions which were censured by ecclesiastical authority was due partly to his translation into theological and philosophical language, which had an already accepted meaning, of an experience which is really inexpressible and the nature of which can only be suggested to those who have not themselves shared it; but it was not due to any hostility towards traditional philosophy as such. There is probably more traditional philosophy in the thought of Eckhart than in that of the more orthodox Gerson, who was, as we have seen, strongly influenced by Ockhamism.

Eckhart, as is well known, expressed his view of the relation of creatures to God in rather startling propositions and antinomies. For example, all creatures, he says, are pure nothing. Again, the essence or 'spark' or citadel of the soul (a conception which the German mystics took over from earlier writers) is 'uncreated', and the soul, through union with God, is transformed into Him as the bread is transformed into the body of Christ. Further, one can find both in Eckhart and Ruysbroeck a tendency to place the unity of the divine nature above and behind, as it were, the trinity of Persons, and to assert the complete union of the essence of the soul in mystical experience with this supreme ontological unity. His statements about the relation of finite being to God and of the transformation of the soul into God are, as they stand and in their *prima facie* meaning, sometimes theologically unorthodox; and they drew upon themselves ecclesiastical censure. This fact has led some historians to see in him a medieval pantheist, while some Nazi writers even went so far as to see in him the forerunner of a new German religion and philosophy. As a matter of fact, however, Eckhart had sometimes explained his own startling propositions at the very time of their writing or utterance. For example, after saying that creatures have no being he went on to explain his meaning. 'All creatures have no being, as their being depends on the presence of God. If God turned away from creatures for one moment, they would be reduced to nothing.' Again, though he admitted that it is erroneous to say that there is something uncreated in the soul, he protested that his accusers had overlooked the interpretation which he had given of the term 'uncreated' as used in this respect. Again, although he admitted that the comparison of the soul's union with God with transubstantiation was an error, he protested that it was in any case only an analogy. As to the tendency of Eckhart and Ruysbroeck to go behind the trinity of Persons to the divine unity of nature, this is easily explicable if one remembers the influence exercised upon them by the Neo-platonic tradition, as represented, for example, by the writings of the Pseudo-Dionysius. Eckhart lived at a time when exactitude and accuracy of expression was expected; and he not only did not

satisfy this demand but also made paradoxical statements in sermons, a fact which naturally attracted
critical attention. That he was preoccupied with the
problem of synthesis, of the relation of finite to
infinite being and, in particular, of the relation of the
human soul to God, is clear; but there is no real
evidence that the great German preacher ever intended to assert pantheism. His bold antinomies
were little more than ways of throwing into relief the
fundamental problems in connexion with the divine
transcendence and immanence, both of which he
accepted. It might perhaps be intellectually exciting
if one could discover in the Middle Ages a German
transcendental idealist; but I doubt if Eckhart is a
very good candidate for this role, in spite of his censured propositions. And as to the attempts of certain
Nazi writers to annex the eminent Dominican, such
attempts, in my opinion, do not stop short of the
absurd.

2. The propriety of including Nicholas of Cusa in
a book on medieval philosophy is open to question.
The traditional element in his thought is certainly
marked, and this fact affords justification for pushing
him back, as it were, into the Middle Ages, even
though his dates, 1401–64, overlap those of an early
Renaissance figure like Marsilius Ficinus (1433–99).
On the other hand, it is possible to emphasize the
forward-looking elements in his thought and associate him with the beginnings of 'modern' philosophy.
Better still, perhaps, one can take note of the combination of elements in his philosophy and insist that
he was essentially a transition-thinker, assigning him
to the Renaissance. Nevertheless, even if one prefers,
as I do, to regard him as a Renaissance figure, there

is, I think, justification for giving a sketch of his philosophy in a book on medieval philosophy, precisely because of his character as a transition-thinker, a philosopher who had a foot, so to speak, in both the medieval and the post-medieval world. It is always useful to remind oneself of the continuity in the history of philosophy. There was no sudden and abrupt transition from medieval to 'modern' philosophy.

Nicholas Chrypfs or Krebs was born at Cusa on the Moselle and was educated as a boy by the Brethren of the Common Life at Deventer. After studying at the universities of Heidelberg and Padua he took the doctorate in law. Later, however, he turned to theology and was ordained priest. Although he was associated at first with the conciliar party and assisted at the Council of Bâle, he later changed his views and became a champion of the position of the Holy See. He fulfilled various missions on behalf of the Holy See, being sent, for example, to Byzantium in connexion with the reunion of the Eastern Church with Rome, which was accomplished at the Council of Florence. In 1448 he was created cardinal and in 1450 he was appointed bishop of Brixen. He died at Todi in Umbria in 1464.

Like Leibniz, Nicholas of Cusa was inspired by the idea of synthesis, of the reconciliation of differences and oppositions. At no time had he any sympathy with the threatened rift in the unity of Christendom; and his belief in the unity of the Church and in the unity of the empire, and in a balance between the two powers was thoroughly medieval, linking him with, for example, Dante; and so also was his simultaneous dislike of despotism and anarchy. For instance, his ideal of the empire was not that of a centralized despotism which would override the rights of individual monarchs and princes, but rather that of a confederation of Christian powers. But, though a champion of the medieval ideal of unity, he was alive to contemporary requirements. Thus, it was his ardent desire for reform which for a time attracted him to the conciliar party, though, quite apart from more theological considerations, he soon became convinced that the desired goal would not be achieved though the conciliar movement, which was more likely to end in anarchy.

The central idea of Nicholas of Cusa's speculative philosophy is that of the synthesis or identity of opposites (*coincidentia oppositorum*). In finite beings we find distinctions and oppositions. For example, in all finite beings essence and existence are distinct. In infinite being, God, however, essence and existence coincide. This was, of course, a tenet of Thomism; but for Nicholas it was a general principle that the oppositions and distinctions of creatures coincide in God. This idea may remind one of Schelling's 'philosophy of identity', that is, of that phase of his philosophical development in which Schelling looked on the Absolute as the vanishing-point of all differences; and there are, indeed, resemblances between the philosophy of the fifteenth-century cardinal and the nineteenth-century German idealist. But, in spite of language which gave rise to some misunderstanding, Nicholas's philosophy was definitely theistic in character.

In asserting the identity of opposites in God, Nicholas did not mean to imply that by juggling with terms and simply stating the identity of opposed or

distinct predicates one can achieve an adequate
positive understanding of God. His point was rather
this. We come to know a finite thing by relating it to
what is already known; we compare it with the already
known, noting similarities and distinctions. Finite
things differ, and must differ, from one another in
various ways; and through experience of finite things
we come to have a number of distinct concepts. But
no one of these concepts can express adequately the
nature of the infinite. All finite things mirror the
infinite; and their distinct attributes must be found
identified in the infinite. On the other hand, as all
our concepts are founded on experience of creatures
and reflect that experience, no one concept is applicable to God in a univocal sense. What the identity of
opposites in the infinite actually is cannot be posi-
tively apprehended by the discursive reason, which
can only approach towards its apprehension as the
ideal term of a process. Nicholas thus asserts the
primacy of the 'negative way'; but if we wish to call
this 'agnosticism' it is not an agnosticism which
results from a refusal to make an intellectual effort,
but rather an agnosticism which results from the progressive realization of God's infinity and transcendence. 'Ignorance' it may be; but it is, in Nicholas's
phrase, 'learned' or 'instructed ignorance'. It is only
by the effort to understand God that we come to
realize that God transcends our understanding. The
infinite is not an object which is proportionate to the
discursive reason. If, says Nicholas, one goes on
adding sides to a polygon inscribed in a circle, the
polygon may approximate more and more to coincid-
ing with the circle; but it will never actually coincide
with the circle, however many sides we may add.

Similarly, the discursive reason may approach the infinite in many ways and approximate to a positive understanding; but it will never achieve it, for the discursive reason, which feeds, as it were, on the distinctions and similarities found in creatures, is incommensurable with the infinite. The discursive reason (*ratio*) is governed by the principle of the incompatibility or mutual exclusion of opposites; but intellect (*intellectus*) transcends this sphere. It follows, however, that language, which is fitted to express the affirmations and denials of the discursive reason, cannot provide an adequate expression of the intuition of the unity of opposites in God. It is employed, therefore, to suggest meaning, rather than to state it clearly; and Nicholas makes use of analogies from mathematics to suggest his meaning.

The world is a theophany, a sensible appearance of God: it is a 'contraction' of the divine. In the 'unfolding' of God in creation absolute unity is 'contracted' into multiplicity; infinity into finitude; eternity into succession; necessity into contingency or possibility. Nicholas is willing to speak of every creature as a 'finite infinity or a created God'. This way of speaking betrays the influence of John Scotus Eriugena. But, though the world consists of finite beings, there is a sense in which it may be called infinite. For the world is potentially infinite, in the sense that it is, in principle, indeterminate in respect of spatio-temporal limits. This conception of the world as the endless unfolding of the divine infinity links Nicholas's philosophy with the systems of Giordano Bruno and Spinoza; but Nicholas did not mean to deny creation.

It is interesting to observe that Nicholas's idea of the world's infinity led him to reject the notion of fixed points in the universe. There is no absolute 'up' or 'down' or 'centre'. The earth is neither the centre of the universe nor its lowest part; nor is it stationary; but no more does the sun possess any privileged position. Our judgements in these matters are relative. Nicholas's abandonment of geocentricism was not a novelty. And when he observed that the account of creation in the Pentateuch was couched in language adapted to the intelligence of readers and was not meant to be a scientific statement, to be taken with absolute literalness, he was repeating what Nicholas of Oresme had already said. But none the less his view of the world was in several respects more akin to those advanced by Renaissance thinkers than to that which was prevalent in the Middle Ages. One may add, by the way, that his mathematical speculations proved a stimulus to Leonardo da Vinci.

I have mentioned that Nicholas's idea of the infinite system of nature was developed by Giordano Bruno and kindred thinkers, though Bruno, and after him Spinoza, developed it in a manner which was alien to Nicholas's fundamentally orthodox Christian standpoint. But his idea of the self-unfolding system of nature as a progressive manifestation of God links him also with Leibniz. So, too, does the following aspect of his thought. The idea of nature as the manifestation of God and of a hierarchy of levels in nature was not, of course, anything new; but Nicholas laid particular emphasis on individual things as particular 'contractions' of the infinite. Each individual thing manifests God in a particular way; and from this it follows that no two individual things are exactly alike. But these individual things form none the less a harmonious system or order, in which individual creatures, none of which are exactly alike, are related to each other. These two ideas of the unique character of each individual thing and of the relation of each individual thing to every other individual thing, are found again in the philosophy of Leibniz.

Finally, although every thing mirrors the universe in some sense, this is particularly true of man, who combines in himself matter, organic life, sensitive animal life, and spiritual intelligence. Man is thus the microcosm, the finite and imperfect representation of the divine identity of opposites. In virtue of his highest rational faculty man can transcend the level of the discursive reason, replace the dialectical operation of that reason by mathematical symbolism, and apprehend in some way the nature of God as the identity of opposites. Beyond this lie supernatural faith and mystical experience, which are open to man only through Christ, the God-Man, who, uniting in Himself the highest and the lowest, is the perfect manifestation of the identity of opposites. Thus man can realize his highest potentialities only through incorporation with Christ in His mystical body, the Church. Nicholas of Cusa's thought was deeply rooted in Catholic theology and spirituality.

Even a very summary sketch of his philosophy shows, I think, the two aspects of Nicholas's thought. For the main lines of his metaphysic he depended very largely on the Pseudo-Dionysius and other writers of the Neo-platonic tradition, though he was influenced too, of course, by later medieval thinkers like Eckhart. For Ockhamism he had scant sympathy. It might appear at first sight perhaps that the net result of what he has to say on our philosophic knowledge of God was not very different from the philosophic scepticism of the nominalists; but the reasons he gives for his attitude on this matter are those given by the Pseudo-Dionysius rather than those given by Ockham. Moreover, in his later writings Nicholas tended to modify his philosophic agnosticism by depicting God as power, which is revealed in the powers and potentialities of creatures. Just as the power of Plato's or Aristotle's mind is revealed in their works, so is God revealed in the powers of finite things. In any case Nicholas developed a large-scale metaphysical system; and this is a fact which differentiates him sharply from the Ockhamists, especially in view of his dependence on the Platonic, or Neo-platonic, tradition. On the other hand, his view of nature as a dynamic self-unfolding system, his abandonment of geocentricism, the emphasis he lays on the individual finite thing and the importance he attaches to mathematical analogy (however much his attitude in this matter may have been suggested by Platonist writers) make his system a forerunner of those philosophies of nature which were one of the leading characteristics of the Renaissance. His insistence on the conception of nature as the potentially infinite, as the created infinite, if one may so express it, and as the 'contraction' or self-unfolding of God on the plane of created existence, together with the idea of nature as an intelligible and harmonious system, obviously implied that nature is a worthy and fit object of study for its own sake. It was philosophies like that of

Nicholas of Cusa, rather than philosophies like that of William of Ockham, which actually formed the mental background of the age in which the great scientists of the Renaissance lived and worked.

CHAPTER XII

POLITICAL PHILOSOPHY

1. POLITICAL philosophy obviously involves reflection on concrete political institutions and issues; and it is inevitably coloured to a greater or lesser extent by recent historical developments and by the circumstances of the time. In medieval political theory it is only natural that one should find a reflection of the changing relations of the spiritual and temporal powers. The existence of two types of society, the Church and the empire or the State, was the historical datum in medieval Europe which formed the subject of a good deal, though certainly not all, of the political reflections of the medieval thinkers. But one can see the same theme, though presented in rather a different form from that in which it was presented in the Middle Ages, in the philosophy of St. Augustine.

St. Augustine tended to look on the State as the embodiment of the spiritual city of Babylon, as something 'worldly' in a disparaging sense. Convinced that the history of mankind is fundamentally the dialectic of good and evil, love of God and hatred of God, he tended to regard the State as the fruit of sin, as an instrument of force which would not have been necessary if man had not sinned. Given man's fallen nature, the State is, indeed, a necessary institution; but, even if the concrete State cannot be simply identified with the spiritual conception of the city of Babylon (the spiritual fellowship of all these who

166

worship self to the exclusion of God), it is so per-
meated with injustice that only the Christian State
can be considered just. In thinking in this way
Augustine was influenced, of course, by what he
knew of the history of States like Assyria, Babylon,
and pagan Rome. The State, endowed with the
power of coercion, is a necessary result of original and
actual sin; but no State can be a truly just society
unless it is a Christian State, informed by principles
which are derived from a higher source than the
State itself. From this it follows, of course, that the
Church is a society which is superior to the State in
point of value and dignity, a doctrine which played
an important part in the Middle Ages. It must be
added, however, that the conviction that the Church
is superior in value to the State is a conviction which
is inseparable from the belief that Christ instituted a
definite Church as the means of securing to man his
eternal salvation: it is not dependent on Augustine's
philosophy of history, even if Augustine's treatment
of the theme of the State's relation to the Church
exercised a considerable influence on subsequent
theory. The claims of the Church to independence,
and the struggle to make these claims effective, were
a logical consequence of the belief that man has a
supernatural and eternal end and that it is through
active membership of the Church that this end is
attained.

  2. This is not to say, however, that Augustine's
pessimistic and low idea of the State was the idea
which actually prevailed in the Middle Ages. Though
he would certainly agree with much of what Augustine had to say about historical States, St. Thomas's
attitude towards the State was different from that of

St. Augustine. For one thing, the historical conditions in which the two men respectively lived were very different: it is not to be expected that a philosopher living in the Christian society of medieval Europe should regard the State in precisely that light in which it was regarded by Augustine, who, although he lived in the last days of the Christian Roman Empire, could not forget the treatment meted out to Christians before the time of Constantine. But even though historical considerations of this sort are important, I want to pass over them and to emphasize rather a more theoretical aspect of the matter. Aquinas was naturally influenced by the writings of canonists and jurists and by the somewhat rudimentary political theories advanced by earlier medieval authors; but the point to which I wish to draw attention is the influence exercised on his political theory by the philosophy of Aristotle.

In accordance with the teaching of Aristotle, Aquinas maintained, not only that society in general is natural to man, but that organized political or civil society is a natural society. That society is natural to man can be shown in several ways. Language, for example, is a social phenomenon and expresses man's social nature. But, if society is a natural institution, so also is organized government a natural institution. Even if men never sinned, there would still be need for some control over their activities directed to the common good. In short, a civil society and civil government are natural institutions in the sense that they are necessary for the fulfilment of men's natural needs and for the leading of a full human life: there is no essential connexion between the State and sin, and man would still have required the State even if he had never fallen. Further, if the State is a natural institution, it is willed by God, the Author of nature.

St. Thomas followed the Aristotelian conception of the State, in distinction from the family, as a self-sufficing community, that is, as a society which possesses in itself all the means requisite for attaining its end, which in this case is the common good of the citizens. By 'common good', he did not mean simply their temporal welfare in the material sense, but, more fully, the leading of the good life, which is defined, in Aristotelian fashion, as a life according to virtue. But, though he held that the State is a self-sufficing or 'perfect' community, he was, unlike Aristotle, a Christian; and he believed that the Church is also a perfect, a self-sufficing community, possessing in itself all the means requisite for attaining its supernatural end, the eternal happiness of its members in the beatific vision of God. At first sight it might appear that Aquinas would go on to say that the State exists to secure the attainment of man's temporal final end, while the Church exists to secure the attainment of man's supernatural final end. But he could not say precisely this; for he was convinced, as a Christian, that man has only one final end, a supernatural one. He held, indeed, that the State has its own sphere (otherwise it could not possibly be a 'perfect' community); but he had to say that the monarch, in his direction of human and earthly affairs, should facilitate the attainment of man's supernatural end. This is a more important point than might perhaps appear. On the one hand, St. Thomas's Aristotelianism rendered any complete subordination of the State to the Church or any

tendency to regard the monarch as no more than a
kind of employee of the Church quite foreign to his
thought. On the other hand, if man has one final end,
a supernatural end, which is primarily cared for by
the Church, it follows that the Church is a superior
society. The State is a natural institution, possessing
its own sphere, the common good in the temporal
order; but there cannot be a complete and absolute
separation between the sphere of the State and that
of the Church, since man has been placed in this world
to secure a supernatural end; and his temporal life
must be directed to the attainment of that end. The
Church is, therefore, superior in dignity to the State;
and if any clash occurs between man's supernatural
interests and what appear to be his temporal
interests, the latter must be subordinated to the
former. The Church has, then, to use later terms, an
indirect power over the State. But it does not possess
a direct power over the State, for the State is not a
department of the Church: it is a natural institution,
and as such it is willed by God.

St. Thomas's Christianity modified, then, his Aristotelian conception of the State. Sometimes he speaks
of the individual as being ordered to the community
as a part to a whole and of the private good of the
individual as being subordinated to the common
good; but his Christian conception of the individual,
as a spiritual person whose final end is supernatural,
rendered any complete subordination of the individual to the State entirely unacceptable. Anything
savouring of political 'totalitarianism' was quite out
of the question for Aquinas, as for any other
Christian medieval thinker. Nor, of course, could
there be any question in his philosophy of the

monarch possessing unlimited power. He shared the
medieval dislike of despotism; and his ideas of the
form of government were flexible. That form of
government is best which will best serve the common
good. In practice this means, for St. Thomas, what
we would call limited or constitutional monarchy.
In any case, however, his philosophy of law, which
was briefly considered in Chapter VI, ruled out any
acceptance of unbridled despotism as legitimate. If
the task of human positive law is to define and apply
the natural law which is itself an expression of the
divine eternal law; if it in any case must be in accordance with the natural moral law; and if it is not
entitled to contradict or disregard the divine positive
law; it follows that the monarch is not, and cannot be,
the fount of morality. On the contrary, he is himself
bound in his public, as in his private, acts by the
objective moral law. Government is willed by God;
but the government has a trust to fulfil; and deposi-
tion of a tyrant is legitimate. Neither for Aristotle
nor for St. Thomas does the State stand beyond good
and evil; but the self-sufficing character of the State
necessarily meant something more for the Greek
philosopher than it did for the Christian theologian.

3. St. Thomas's ideal of the two spheres and of the
balance of the two powers was shared by the great
medieval poet Dante (1265–1321). But, though
Dante's period of literary activity fell well after St.
Thomas's death, he was much more concerned with
the idea of the empire than St. Thomas had been.
This fact is easily explicable in terms of the conditions of Dante's life. The Italian poet was a witness
of the effects of the quarrels between papacy and
empire; and he was involved in the factions between

the papal and imperial parties. He naturally tended
to think, therefore, in terms of Church and empire;
and in his book *On Monarchy* (*De monarchia*) he
defended the imperial cause. He argued that temporal monarchy, in the sense of a universal empire, is
necessary to the well-being of man. There must be a
supreme temporal judge and ruler if peace and freedom are to be attained. Dante idealized the empire;
and he disregarded, or did not realize, the fact that
the medieval empire, which had never really been a
universal monarchy, even within Christendom, was
becoming less and less of an effective reality. Dante
also tried to show that imperial authority derives
immediately from God, and that the emperor has no
human superior. At the same time, even if his
sympathies were with the emperor, while St. Thomas's
had been with the pope, Dante made no attempt to
deny the spiritual jurisdiction of the papacy; and his
philosophical principles were more or less those of
St. Thomas. He shared Aquinas's Christian view of
man and his destiny; he recognized the two powers
and the two spheres; and his idealization of the
empire and his derivation of the emperor's authority
directly from God were not designed to promote
monarchic despotism or tyranny. The practical
reason why he espoused the imperial cause was his
belief that only through the empire as he conceived
it could peace be attained. The realization of this
peace was, in his opinion, prevented by the papacy's
insistence on temporal, as well as spiritual jurisdiction, and by its political policy. From the theoretical
point of view he subscribed to the teaching of Pope
Gelasius I that neither the spiritual nor the temporal
power should attempt to usurp the function of the

other. This was, of course, the view of St. Thomas also.

4. This theory of the two powers or two swords was the common theory of the early Middle Ages and of the thirteenth century; but in the thirteenth century a tendency to explain away or eviscerate the theory became visible, even though it was verbally accepted. Popes like Innocent III and Innocent IV had exalted the papal power and sovereignty in both theory and practice; but the extreme statement of the papal claims was that of Boniface VIII in his cele-brated Bull, *Unam Sanctam* (1302). Boniface did not deny the theory of the two powers; but he insisted that though the temporal sword should not actually be wielded by the Church it is wielded by temporal monarchs only in subordination to the Church. The spiritual power is judge of the temporal; but the spiritual power can be judged only by God. In face of the remonstrances of the king of France, Boniface replied that he had not intended to usurp the power of monarchs or to assert the Church's direct control over temporal affairs. He had, however, read and utilized the work of Giles of Rome (*c.* 1246–1316), theologian and philosopher, *On ecclesiastical power.* In this work Giles admitted the theory of two powers and two swords; and he admitted also that the Church ought not to wield the temporal sword. But he made it quite clear that, in his opinion, the Church possesses the temporal power, just as Christ possessed temporal power, though it is not the task of the Church, any more than it was of Christ in His earthly life, to exercise the temporal power directly. Accord-ing to Giles of Rome, then, the Church possesses jurisdiction in temporal as well as in spiritual affairs,

even if the direct exercise of temporal power is entrusted to monarchs and princes.

5. This sort of view naturally aroused opposition.
For example, a Dominican known as Jean Quidort
and also as John of Paris, defended the independent
authority of the monarch in his work *On Royal and
Papal Power* (1302–3). Being concerned immediately
with the cause of the king of France, he took pains
to show that, though the Church is essentially universal or catholic, universality, even of principle, is
not required in order that a political community
should be a self-sufficing autonomous unit, fulfilling
the definition of a State. Nor can any good historical
reason be adduced for saying that the king of France
is subject to or derives his authority from the emperor. The question whether or not the French
monarch was subject to the emperor was not, however, a practical problem; and John's interest centred
round the relation of king to pope and of the State
to the Church. Basing his views on Aristotle and St.
Thomas, he argued that the autonomous political
community existed before Christ's institution of the
Church. It has its roots in human nature itself,
which was created by God; and it possesses a moral
justification of its own. Civil government, too, is
natural. It has always been found in political com-
munities; and it is essential to the well-being of
political society. It follows, therefore, that civil
government does not owe its justification to the
Church. Spiritual authority is, by its nature, higher
in point of dignity than civil authority; but this does
not mean that civil authority derives from or is
essentially subject to spiritual authority. Neither
abstract theory nor historical argument can show

that the king of France, as king of France, is subject
to the pope, even though he is, as a Christian man,
subject to the purely spiritual authority of the
Church.

6. In the thirteenth and at the beginning of the
fourteenth century we find, then, a general acceptance
of the theory of the two powers, which owed its
origin to a combination of theoretical reasoning and
the force of historical facts and developments. No
very profound knowledge of medieval history is
needed, however, in order to realize the unstable
character of the equlibrium between the two powers.
Moreover, it was natural, I think, that divergences of
theory should arise, not simply as a reflection of the
ambitions and practical aims of contending parties
and interests and under the influence of actual historical developments (though these factors have to
be taken into account, of course), but also because
the theory of the two powers, as represented by St.
Thomas, for example, contained within itself the
seeds of those divergences. On the one hand, the
stressing of the primacy of the supernatural, which
was acknowledged by all Christian thinkers, could
easily, given the concrete historical conditions, lead
to or be used in support of the sort of views cham-
pioned by Giles of Rome. In this case the theory
of the two powers, though it was accepted verbally,
was whittled away in favour of the spiritual power.
On the other hand, the Aristotelian elements of
Aquinas's theory, could, if stressed, lead to a whittling
away of the two powers theory in favour of the State;
for Aristotle knew nothing of any supernatural end
or institution and understood the self-sufficing
autonomy of the State in a sense different from

that in which St. Thomas understood it. The fact that the latter development took place was due in large part to the historic evolution of national States in the Middle Ages; but the possibility was contained within the theory itself. We shall see presently how it was realized in fourteenth-century political philosophy.

7. In 1323 Pope John XXII attempted to intervene in an imperial election, maintaining that papal confirmation was required. When Ludwig of Bavaria was elected, the pope denounced the election, but in 1328 Ludwig had himself crowned at Rome. In the ensuing quarrel between the emperor and the papacy William of Ockham took the side of the emperor, at whose court he had sought refuge. He took the line that one would expect, insisting that the imperial power and authority is not derived from the Holy See: it derives from the emperor's election, confirmation of which by the pope is not required. This assertion was not meant, of course, to be restricted to the emperor: Ockham expressly declared that all legitimate sovereigns enjoy an authority which is not derived from the Church.

But Ockham did not assert the temporal monarch's independence, in order to support political absolutism. All men are born free, in the sense that they have a right to freedom; and they enjoy a natural right to choose their rulers, even though political government is a natural necessity. This is not to say that a political community is not entitled to establish a hereditary monarchy, if it chooses; but none the less a monarch's authority rests on the free consent of the people. In the case of the emperor the electors stand as representatives of the people. The people, then, have the right of deposing a monarch who abuses his trust. This view was not, however, a novelty; and it should certainly not be interpreted as involving a denial of the general medieval principle that all authority derives ultimately from God.

But Ockham was not content with asserting the emperor's independence of the papacy: he also turned his attack against the position of the pope within the Church. In his view papal supremacy within the Church was unjustified and detrimental to the good of Christendom. Papal power should be limited by means of a general council. He did not deny that the pope is vicar of Christ and successor of St. Peter; but he called for a constitutional check on what he regarded as unjustified papal absolutism. He envisaged corporations like parishes and monasteries sending representatives to provincial synods, which would in turn elect representatives to sit in a general council, which would act as a check on the exercise of absolute power by the pope. In outlining this plan Ockham may have drawn on his experience and his knowledge of the constitutions of the mendicant Orders. The Dominican, John of Paris, who has been mentioned for his championship of the independent authority of the king of France, had already maintained that a general council can legitimately depose a pope for a grave reason; and he had regarded it as the function of the college of cardinals to limit papal absolutism.

The attack on papal absolutism by John of Paris and William of Ockham may be said to have heralded the conciliar movement which later received such a powerful impetus through the Great Schism (1378–1417). But in spite of this attack Ockham's polemical writings were not revolutionary, as far as political theory is concerned. His thought moved within the medieval framework of papacy and empire; and he was driven to polemics not so much out of any particular love of political theorizing as, first, out of dislike for the attitude of the Holy See in regard to the dispute with a group of Franciscans over evangelical poverty, and, secondly, out of a desire to defend the cause of his patron, Ludwig of Bavaria. In regard to the general acceptance of the two-powers theory he was fundamentally at one with other medieval theologians and philosophers. For a more revolutionary attitude we must turn to Marsilius of Padua, the author of the celebrated *Defender of peace* (*Defensor pacis*).

8. Marsilius's exact dates are not known; but he was rector of the university of Paris for a time (1312–13). Apparently he afterwards returned to Italy and studied 'natural philosophy'; but before very long he was back in Paris, where he wrote his *Defensor pacis*, probably in collaboration with John of Jandun. The book was completed in 1324; and in 1326 Marsilius, together with John of Jandun, took refuge with Ludwig of Bavaria. His views may have been acceptable to his patron; but they met with criticism from Ockham, a criticism to which Marsilius replied in his *Defensor minor*. He died before 1343, as Pope Clement VI spoke of him in the April of that year as already dead.

In considering Marsilius of Padua's political theory it is necessary to bear in mind the concrete historical condition of contemporary northern Italy. The

principalities and city-republics of northern Italy
were wrecked by factions and wars, with all their
accompanying evils. In Marsilius's interpretation of
the situation this condition of affairs was primarily
due to papal policy and claims and to the disturbance
of peace by the interference of ecclesiastical authority
in matters of State, wielding the weapons of excommunication and interdict. The point is not so much
whether Marsilius's interpretation of the contemporary Italian scene was true or false, adequate or
inadequate, one-sided or just, as that the historic
situation, as he saw and interpreted it, was reflected
in his political theory. When we read of his enthusiasm for the autonomous State and notice his comparative disregard of the empire, we should realize
that this was due not so much to 'modernity' as to a
passionate devotion to the cause of the small city-
republic of northern Italy. And his enmity towards
the papacy was due in large part to his interpretation of the evils of northern Italy. Naturally, his
theoretic treatment of the issues involved possesses
an importance which extends beyond a mere interpretation of the contemporary scene; but all
the same it is well to bear in mind the historic
factors which influenced the direction of his thought,
as this helps to prevent one from over-modernizing
him.

The State is a perfect or self-sufficing community,
which was originally brought into being for the sake
of life, but which has as its end the promotion of the
good life. In this conception of the State and its function Marsilius follows Aristotle; but he at once shows
the direction of his thought by including the priesthood, even the Christian priesthood, as a part of the

State. In the course of his book it becomes quite clear that he is not content simply with rejecting ecclesiastical interference in temporal affairs, but that he is intent on subordinating the Church to the State. His position was thus, to use a later term, frankly 'Erastian', provided that the term is not understood to mean that Marsilius was a Protestant before Protestantism. He devotes a good deal of space to examining and rejecting, in a very high-handed manner, the claims of the Church, and especially of the papacy, to independent jurisdiction; but his religious controversy was undertaken in what he regarded as the true interests of the State, rather than out of religious or theological convictions. It is this fact which has led some writers to speak of Marsilius's political theory as 'Averroistic' in character. But there does not appear to be any very good reason for speaking of his theory as specifically 'Averroistic', although he was certainly in touch with thinkers like John of Jandun who were animated by the Averroistic veneration for Aristotle. Marsilius considered that it was the Church's claims and activities which disturbed and prevented the peace of the State; and he found the key to his problem in the Aristotelian idea of the autonomous State, which he interpreted as involving the subordination of the Church to the State. Marsilius thus developed the Aristotelian side of medieval political theory in such a way as to destroy the other side, the insistence on the independent spiritual power.

In defence of his main aim Marsilius developed the philosophy of law in a new direction. In the Thomist scheme the different types of law are closely linked together, for the law of the State is based on the

natural law, while the natural law is an expression of
the eternal law of God, who is the ultimate source of
all law. Marsilius, however, tended to divorce
human positive law, in the sense of the law of the
State, from its relation to the natural law. He did not
deny that there is such a thing as natural law; but he
distinguishes two types of natural law. The phrase
'natural law' may refer to those laws which are
enacted in all nations and the obligatory character of
which is practically taken for granted. On the other
hand, 'there are certain people who call "natural law"
the dictates of right reason in regard to human acts,
and natural law in this sense they subsume under
divine law'. But in these two descriptions of natural
law the phrase 'natural law' is used equivocally.
Why? The answer brings us to the heart of the
matter. Marsilius defined law in the strict sense as a
preceptive and coercive rule, fortified by sanctions
applicable in this life. But in this case it is human
positive law, in the sense of the law of the State,
which is law in the strict sense. Natural law, understood in the second sense mentioned above, is not
law in the strict sense. A dictate of right reason becomes, of course, law in the strict sense if it is
embodied in a law of the State, furnished with sanctions in this life; but, if it is considered simply as a
moral law, the sanctions of which are applicable in
the next life, it is law only in an equivocal sense. From
this it follows that the law of Christ is not properly
speaking 'law'; it is more akin, says Marsilius, to the
prescriptions of a doctor. Further, the law of the
Church cannot be law in the strict sense; for it is, of
itself, furnished only with spiritual sanctions. If it
is furnished with temporal sanctions, fully applicable

in this life, it owes this fact to the permission and will of the State; and it thus becomes State law. Now, Marsilius did sometimes say, in a rather conventional manner, that if divine and human laws clash it is the former which should be obeyed; but he also maintained the idea that it is the State alone which is competent to judge whether a given law is consonant with the divine law or not. One can say, then, that even if he did not deny outright the Thomist conception of natural law and of its relation to the law of the State, he nevertheless to all intents and purposes, divorced the law of the State from its metaphysical foundation and norms. It is only the law of the State which is law in the proper sense and it is only the temporal legislator who is a legislator in the proper sense. The Church law is not law in the proper sense; and the spiritual legislator is not a legislator in the proper sense. It follows not only that the extreme claims of popes like Boniface VIII lack all justification, but also that the common medieval conception of ecclesiastical jurisdiction is wrong. There is no sacerdotal jurisdiction in the proper sense of the word. Canon law was simply brushed aside by Marsilius.

Who is the temporal legislator? The primary efficient cause of law is the people, or at least the more weighty part (*pars valentior*) of the people. This more weighty part need not be a numerical majority; but it must be legitimately representative of the people. As it is difficult in practice, however, for the whole body of citizens to draw up laws, it is suitable if a committee or commission formulates laws and then proposes them to the legislator for acceptance or rejection. The office of the prince is to

apply and enforce the laws. The executive is thus
subordinate to the legislature; and this subordination
is best expressed in practice if each prince or government is elected. This is not necessary, but, in itself,
election is preferable to hereditary succession. It has
been maintained that Marsilius envisaged a clear
separation of powers in the State; but, though he
distinguished the executive from the legislature, he
subordinated the judiciary power to the executive.
Further, although he admitted in a sense the
sovereignty of the people, he made no explicit
statement of a social contract theory.[1] His subordination of the executive to the legislature was
dictated by practical considerations concerning the
well-being of the State rather than by any philosophic theory of a social contract. He was concerned above all with peace; and he saw that
tyranny and despotism were not conducive to peace
within the State.

I mentioned earlier that one should bear in mind
Marsilius's preoccupation with problems of contemporary Italy. At the same time, however, it is undeniable that, as seen in the light of subsequent
history, Marsilius's political theory foreshadows the
growth of the State of a later age. In the period of
transition and formation between the fall of the
Roman Empire and the establishment of the Western
civilization of medieval times the Church had been
the great unifying factor. In the early Middle Ages
the idea of the empire, if not the reality, was still

---

[1] The theory that political society originated in a compact
of some sort between the members had been implied by, for
example, John of Paris. As to the theory of a compact or
contract between citizens and ruler, this can be found as early
as the eleventh century in Manegold of Lautenbach.

strong; and the theory of the two powers won general acceptance. This theory was also applicable to temporal powers like England, which never had any real connexion with the medieval empire. But during the Middle Ages strong and consolidated States were growing up, as the effective power of monarchs like the king of France gradually increased. The period of the great absolute monarchies lay still in the future, but the gradual emergence of national self-consciousness was a historical fact which corresponded, on the plane of theory, to that development of the Aristotelian element in medieval political philosophy which we find in the writings of a Marsilius of Padua. Marsilius may have concentrated on an attack on the papacy and ecclesiastical jurisdiction within the medieval setting, and it was in this light that he was understood in the fourteenth century; but his work looked forward to the political theory of Hobbes and the historic growth of the modern State. For him it was only the State which is truly a 'perfect society'; the Church's task, as far as this world is concerned, is little more than that of serving the State by creating the moral and spiritual conditions which will facilitate the work of the State.

The medieval ideal of united Christendom was reflected in the thirteenth century in the close association of theology and philosophy and in the commonly accepted political theory of the balance between the two powers, the spiritual and the temporal. In the fourteenth century we find the historic movement towards disintegration reflected in the Ockhamist separation of theology and philosophy and in Marsilius's theory of the autonomous and

fully self-sufficient State. Conversely, the Ockhamist
movement and theories like those of Marsilius of
Padua had their influence in the practical field, by
fostering a spirit which would reach its full development at a later period.

SUGGESTIONS FOR FURTHER READING

1. GENERAL

M. H. Carré   *Realists and Nominalists* (Oxford, 1946).

F. C. Copleston   *A History of Philosophy*, Vol. II. Augustine to Scotus (Burns, Oates, 1950).

C. S. J. Curtis   *A Short History of Western Philosophy in the Middle Ages* (MacDonald, 1950).

M. De Wulf   *History of Mediaeval Philosophy* (Longmans, Vol. I, 1935, Vol. II, 1938, Vol. III is available only in French, Louvain, 1947).

E. Gilson   *La philosophie au moyen âge* (Paris, 1944). *The Spirit of Mediaeval Philosophy* (Sheed and Ward, 1950).

D. J. B. Hawkins   *A Sketch of Mediaeval Philosophy* (Sheed and Ward, 1946).

H. Rashdall   *The Universities of Europe in the Middle Ages* (Edited by F. M. Powicke and A. B. Enden). (Three vols. Oxford, 1936.)

2. ST. AUGUSTINE

A Monument to St. Augustine (Sheed and Ward, 1930. Various authors). Reprinted, 1945.

E. Gilson   *Introduction à l'étude de saint Augustin* (Paris, 1943).

There is a useful sketch of early Christian Philosophy in:

A. H. Armstrong   *An Introduction to Ancient Philosophy* (Methuen, 1947).

3. ST. BONAVENTURE

E. Gilson   *The Philosophy of St. Bonaventure* (Sheed and Ward, 1938).

4. ST. THOMAS AQUINAS

M. C. D'Arcy   *Thomas Aquinas* (Benn, 1931).
E. Gilson   *Le thomisme* (Paris, 1944).
J. Maritain   *St. Thomas Aquinas* (Sheed and Ward, 1946).
R. L. Patterson   *The Concept of God in the Philosophy of Aquinas* (George Allen and Unwin, 1933).
A. D. Sertillanges *Foundations of Thomistic Philosophy* (Sands, 1931).

5. ROGER BACON

J. H. Bridges   *The Life and Work of Roger Bacon* (Williams and Norgate, 1914).

6. JOHN DUNS SCOTUS

C. Harris   *Duns Scotus* (Oxford, 1927. Two vols.). Useful, but makes copious use of an unauthentic work.

7. OCKHAMISM

E. A. Moody   *The Logic of William of Ockham* (Sheed and Ward, 1935).
J. R. Weinberg   *Nicolaus of Autrecourt* (Geoffrey Cumberlege, 1948).

8. NICHOLAS OF CUSA

H. Bett   *Nicholas of Cusa* (Methuen, 1932).

9. POLITICAL PHILOSOPHY

A. P. D'Entrèves   *The Medieval Contribution to Political Thought* (Oxford University Press, 1939).
G. H. Sabine   *History of Political Theory* (Harrap, 1941).

For a fuller bibliography, with lists of texts and studies, see my book mentioned above (1). For much fuller and more detailed bibliographies see the work of De Wulf mentioned above (1) and Uebeweg-Geyer's *Die patristische und scholastische Philosophie* (Berlin, 1928).

INDEX

The names of philosophers and of those who have been mentioned for their philosophical opinions have been printed in capital letters.

A CATALOG OF SELECTED DOVER
BOOKS IN ALL FIELDS OF INTEREST

CONCERNING THE SPIRITUAL IN ART, Wassily Kandinsky. Pioneering work by father of abstract art. Thoughts on color theory, nature of art. Analysis of earlier masters. 12 illustrations. 80pp. of text. 5⅜ x 8½.   23411-8 Pa. $4.95

ANIMALS: 1,419 Copyright-Free Illustrations of Mammals, Birds, Fish, Insects, etc., Jim Harter (ed.). Clear wood engravings present, in extremely lifelike poses, over 1,000 species of animals. One of the most extensive pictorial sourcebooks of its kind. Captions. Index. 284pp. 9 x 12.   23766-4 Pa. $14.95

CELTIC ART: The Methods of Construction, George Bain. Simple geometric techniques for making Celtic interlacements, spirals, Kells-type initials, animals, humans, etc. Over 500 illustrations. 160pp. 9 x 12. (Available in U.S. only.)   22923-8 Pa. $9.95

AN ATLAS OF ANATOMY FOR ARTISTS, Fritz Schider. Most thorough reference work on art anatomy in the world. Hundreds of illustrations, including selections from works by Vesalius, Leonardo, Goya, Ingres, Michelangelo, others. 593 illustrations. 192pp. 7⅛ x 10¼.   20241-0 Pa. $9.95

CELTIC HAND STROKE-BY-STROKE (Irish Half-Uncial from "The Book of Kells"): An Arthur Baker Calligraphy Manual, Arthur Baker. Complete guide to creating each letter of the alphabet in distinctive Celtic manner. Covers hand position, strokes, pens, inks, paper, more. Illustrated. 48pp. 8¼ x 11.   24336-2 Pa. $3.95

EASY ORIGAMI, John Montroll. Charming collection of 32 projects (hat, cup, pelican, piano, swan, many more) specially designed for the novice origami hobbyist. Clearly illustrated easy-to-follow instructions insure that even beginning papercrafters will achieve successful results. 48pp. 8¼ x 11.   27298-2 Pa. $3.50

THE COMPLETE BOOK OF BIRDHOUSE CONSTRUCTION FOR WOODWORKERS, Scott D. Campbell. Detailed instructions, illustrations, tables. Also data on bird habitat and instinct patterns. Bibliography. 3 tables. 63 illustrations in 15 figures. 48pp. 5¼ x 8½.   24407-5 Pa. $2.50

BLOOMINGDALE'S ILLUSTRATED 1886 CATALOG: Fashions, Dry Goods and Housewares, Bloomingdale Brothers. Famed merchants' extremely rare catalog depicting about 1,700 products: clothing, housewares, firearms, dry goods, jewelry, more. Invaluable for dating, identifying vintage items. Also, copyright-free graphics for artists, designers. Co-published with Henry Ford Museum & Greenfield Village. 160pp. 8¼ x 11.   25780-0 Pa. $12.95

HISTORIC COSTUME IN PICTURES, Braun & Schneider. Over 1,450 costumed figures in clearly detailed engravings–from dawn of civilization to end of 19th century. Captions. Many folk costumes. 256pp. 8⅜ x 11¾.   23150-X Pa. $12.95

CATALOG OF DOVER BOOKS

FRANK LLOYD WRIGHT'S DANA HOUSE, Donald Hoffmann. Pictorial essay of residential masterpiece with over 160 interior and exterior photos, plans, elevations, sketches and studies. 128pp. 9¼ x 10¾. 29120-0 Pa. $14.95

THE MALE AND FEMALE FIGURE IN MOTION: 60 Classic Photographic Sequences, Eadweard Muybridge. 60 true-action photographs of men and women walking, running, climbing, bending, turning, etc., reproduced from rare 19th-century masterpiece. vi + 121pp. 9 x 12. 24745-7 Pa. $12.95

1001 QUESTIONS ANSWERED ABOUT THE SEASHORE, N. J. Berrill and Jacquelyn Berrill. Queries answered about dolphins, sea snails, sponges, starfish, fishes, shore birds, many others. Covers appearance, breeding, growth, feeding, much more. 305pp. 5¼ x 8¼. 23366-9 Pa. $9.95

ATTRACTING BIRDS TO YOUR YARD, William J. Weber. Easy-to-follow guide offers advice on how to attract the greatest diversity of birds: birdhouses, feeders, water and waterers, much more. 96pp. 5³⁄₁₆ x 8¼. 28927-3 Pa. $2.50

MEDICINAL AND OTHER USES OF NORTH AMERICAN PLANTS: A Historical Survey with Special Reference to the Eastern Indian Tribes, Charlotte Erichsen-Brown. Chronological historical citations document 500 years of usage of plants, trees, shrubs native to eastern Canada, northeastern U.S. Also complete identifying information. 343 illustrations. 544pp. 6½ x 9¼. 25951-X Pa. $12.95

STORYBOOK MAZES, Dave Phillips. 23 stories and mazes on two-page spreads: Wizard of Oz, Treasure Island, Robin Hood, etc. Solutions. 64pp. 8¼ x 11. 23628-5 Pa. $2.95

AMERICAN NEGRO SONGS: 230 Folk Songs and Spirituals, Religious and Secular, John W. Work. This authoritative study traces the African influences of songs sung and played by black Americans at work, in church, and as entertainment. The author discusses the lyric significance of such songs as "Swing Low, Sweet Chariot," "John Henry," and others and offers the words and music for 230 songs. Bibliography. Index of Song Titles. 272pp. 6½ x 9¼. 40271-1 Pa. $10.95

MOVIE-STAR PORTRAITS OF THE FORTIES, John Kobal (ed.). 163 glamor, studio photos of 106 stars of the 1940s: Rita Hayworth, Ava Gardner, Marlon Brando, Clark Gable, many more. 176pp. 8⅜ x 11¼. 23546-7 Pa. $14.95

BENCHLEY LOST AND FOUND, Robert Benchley. Finest humor from early 30s, about pet peeves, child psychologists, post office and others. Mostly unavailable elsewhere. 73 illustrations by Peter Arno and others. 183pp. 5⅜ x 8½. 22410-4 Pa. $6.95

YEKL and THE IMPORTED BRIDEGROOM AND OTHER STORIES OF YIDDISH NEW YORK, Abraham Cahan. Film Hester Street based on *Yekl* (1896). Novel, other stories among first about Jewish immigrants on N.Y.'s East Side. 240pp. 5⅜ x 8½. 22427-9 Pa. $7.95

SELECTED POEMS, Walt Whitman. Generous sampling from *Leaves of Grass*. Twenty-four poems include "I Hear America Singing," "Song of the Open Road," "I Sing the Body Electric," "When Lilacs Last in the Dooryard Bloom'd," "O Captain! My Captain!"—all reprinted from an authoritative edition. Lists of titles and first lines. 128pp. 5³⁄₁₆ x 8¼. 26878-0 Pa. $1.00

CATALOG OF DOVER BOOKS

MY BONDAGE AND MY FREEDOM, Frederick Douglass. Born a slave, Douglass became outspoken force in antislavery movement. The best of Douglass' autobiographies. Graphic description of slave life. 464pp. 5⅜ x 8½. 22457-0 Pa. $8.95

FOLLOWING THE EQUATOR: A Journey Around the World, Mark Twain. Fascinating humorous account of 1897 voyage to Hawaii, Australia, India, New Zealand, etc. Ironic, bemused reports on peoples, customs, climate, flora and fauna, politics, much more. 197 illustrations. 720pp. 5⅜ x 8½. 26113-1 Pa. $15.95

THE PEOPLE CALLED SHAKERS, Edward D. Andrews. Definitive study of Shakers: origins, beliefs, practices, dances, social organization, furniture and crafts, etc. 33 illustrations. 351pp. 5⅜ x 8½. 21081-2 Pa. $12.95

THE MYTHS OF GREECE AND ROME, H. A. Guerber. A classic of mythology, generously illustrated, long prized for its simple, graphic, accurate retelling of the principal myths of Greece and Rome, and for its commentary on their origins and significance. With 64 illustrations by Michelangelo, Raphael, Titian, Rubens, Canova, Bernini and others. 480pp. 5⅜ x 8½. 27584-1 Pa. $10.95

PSYCHOLOGY OF MUSIC, Carl E. Seashore. Classic work discusses music as a medium from psychological viewpoint. Clear treatment of physical acoustics, auditory apparatus, sound perception, development of musical skills, nature of musical feeling, host of other topics. 88 figures. 408pp. 5⅜ x 8½. 21851-1 Pa. $11.95

THE PHILOSOPHY OF HISTORY, Georg W. Hegel. Great classic of Western thought develops concept that history is not chance but rational process, the evolution of freedom. 457pp. 5⅜ x 8½. 20112-0 Pa. $9.95

THE BOOK OF TEA, Kakuzo Okakura. Minor classic of the Orient: entertaining, charming explanation, interpretation of traditional Japanese culture in terms of tea ceremony. 94pp. 5⅜ x 8½. 20070-1 Pa. $3.95

LIFE IN ANCIENT EGYPT, Adolf Erman. Fullest, most thorough, detailed older account with much not in more recent books, domestic life, religion, magic, medicine, commerce, much more. Many illustrations reproduce tomb paintings, carvings, hieroglyphs, etc. 597pp. 5⅜ x 8½. 22632-8 Pa. $12.95

SUNDIALS, Their Theory and Construction, Albert Waugh. Far and away the best, most thorough coverage of ideas, mathematics concerned, types, construction, adjusting anywhere. Simple, nontechnical treatment allows even children to build several of these dials. Over 100 illustrations. 230pp. 5⅜ x 8½. 22947-5 Pa. $8.95

THEORETICAL HYDRODYNAMICS, L. M. Milne-Thomson. Classic exposition of the mathematical theory of fluid motion, applicable to both hydrodynamics and aerodynamics. Over 600 exercises. 768pp. 6⅛ x 9¼. 68970-0 Pa. $20.95

SONGS OF EXPERIENCE: Facsimile Reproduction with 26 Plates in Full Color, William Blake. 26 full-color plates from a rare 1826 edition. Includes "The Tyger," "London," "Holy Thursday," and other poems. Printed text of poems. 48pp. 5¼ x 7. 24636-1 Pa. $4.95

OLD-TIME VIGNETTES IN FULL COLOR, Carol Belanger Grafton (ed.). Over 390 charming, often sentimental illustrations, selected from archives of Victorian graphics—pretty women posing, children playing, food, flowers, kittens and puppies, smiling cherubs, birds and butterflies, much more. All copyright-free. 48pp. 9¼ x 12¼. 27269-9 Pa. $9.95

PIANO TUNING, J. Cree Fischer. Clearest, best book for beginner, amateur. Simple repairs, raising dropped notes, tuning by easy method of flattened fifths. No previous skills needed. 4 illustrations. 201pp. 5⅜ x 8½. 23267-0 Pa. $6.95

HINTS TO SINGERS, Lillian Nordica. Selecting the right teacher, developing confidence, overcoming stage fright, and many other important skills receive thoughtful discussion in this indispensible guide, written by a world-famous diva of four decades' experience. 96pp. 5³/₈ x 8¹/₂. 40094-8 Pa. $4.95

THE COMPLETE NONSENSE OF EDWARD LEAR, Edward Lear. All nonsense limericks, zany alphabets, Owl and Pussycat, songs, nonsense botany, etc., illustrated by Lear. Total of 320pp. 5⅜ x 8½. (Available in U.S. only.) 20167-8 Pa. $7.95

VICTORIAN PARLOUR POETRY: An Annotated Anthology, Michael R. Turner. 117 gems by Longfellow, Tennyson, Browning, many lesser-known poets. "The Village Blacksmith," "Curfew Must Not Ring Tonight," "Only a Baby Small," dozens more, often difficult to find elsewhere. Index of poets, titles, first lines. xxiii + 325pp. 5⅝ x 8¼. 27044-0 Pa. $12.95

DUBLINERS, James Joyce. Fifteen stories offer vivid, tightly focused observations of the lives of Dublin's poorer classes. At least one, "The Dead," is considered a masterpiece. Reprinted complete and unabridged from standard edition. 160pp. 5³⁄₁₆ x 8¼. 26870-5 Pa. $1.50

GREAT WEIRD TALES: 14 Stories by Lovecraft, Blackwood, Machen and Others, S. T. Joshi (ed.). 14 spellbinding tales, including "The Sin Eater," by Fiona McLeod, "The Eye Above the Mantel," by Frank Belknap Long, as well as renowned works by R. H. Barlow, Lord Dunsany, Arthur Machen, W. C. Morrow and eight other masters of the genre. 256pp. 5⅜ x 8½. (Available in U.S. only.) 40436-6 Pa. $8.95

THE BOOK OF THE SACRED MAGIC OF ABRAMELIN THE MAGE, translated by S. MacGregor Mathers. Medieval manuscript of ceremonial magic. Basic document in Aleister Crowley, Golden Dawn groups. 268pp. 5⅜ x 8½. 23211-5 Pa. $9.95

NEW RUSSIAN-ENGLISH AND ENGLISH-RUSSIAN DICTIONARY, M. A. O'Brien. This is a remarkably handy Russian dictionary, containing a surprising amount of information, including over 70,000 entries. 366pp. 4½ x 6⅛. 20208-9 Pa. $10.95

HISTORIC HOMES OF THE AMERICAN PRESIDENTS, Second, Revised Edition, Irvin Haas. A traveler's guide to American Presidential homes, most open to the public, depicting and describing homes occupied by every American President from George Washington to George Bush. With visiting hours, admission charges, travel routes. 175 photographs. Index. 160pp. 8¼ x 11. 26751-2 Pa. $13.95

NEW YORK IN THE FORTIES, Andreas Feininger. 162 brilliant photographs by the well-known photographer, formerly with *Life* magazine. Commuters, shoppers, Times Square at night, much else from city at its peak. Captions by John von Hartz. 181pp. 9¼ x 10¾. 23585-8 Pa. $13.95

INDIAN SIGN LANGUAGE, William Tomkins. Over 525 signs developed by Sioux and other tribes. Written instructions and diagrams. Also 290 pictographs. 111pp. 6⅛ x 9¼. 22029-X Pa. $3.95

PHOTOGRAPHIC SKETCHBOOK OF THE CIVIL WAR, Alexander Gardner. 100 photos taken on field during the Civil War. Famous shots of Manassas Harper's Ferry, Lincoln, Richmond, slave pens, etc. 244pp. 10⅝ x 8¼. 22731-6 Pa. $10.95

FIVE ACRES AND INDEPENDENCE, Maurice G. Kains. Great back-to-the-land classic explains basics of self-sufficient farming. The one book to get. 95 illustrations. 397pp. 5⅜ x 8½. 20974-1 Pa. $7.95

SONGS OF EASTERN BIRDS, Dr. Donald J. Borror. Songs and calls of 60 species most common to eastern U.S.: warblers, woodpeckers, flycatchers, thrushes, larks, many more in high-quality recording. Cassette and manual 99912-2 $9.95

A MODERN HERBAL, Margaret Grieve. Much the fullest, most exact, most useful compilation of herbal material. Gigantic alphabetical encyclopedia, from aconite to zedoary, gives botanical information, medical properties, folklore, economic uses, much else. Indispensable to serious reader. 161 illustrations. 888pp. 6½ x 9¼. 2-vol. set. (Available in U.S. only.) Vol. I: 22798-7 Pa. $10.95
Vol. II: 22799-5 Pa. $10.95

HIDDEN TREASURE MAZE BOOK, Dave Phillips. Solve 34 challenging mazes accompanied by heroic tales of adventure. Evil dragons, people-eating plants, blood-thirsty giants, many more dangerous adversaries lurk at every twist and turn. 34 mazes, stories, solutions. 48pp. 8¼ x 11. 24566-7 Pa. $2.95

LETTERS OF W. A. MOZART, Wolfgang A. Mozart. Remarkable letters show bawdy wit, humor, imagination, musical insights, contemporary musical world; includes some letters from Leopold Mozart. 276pp. 5⅜ x 8½. 22859-2 Pa. $9.95

BASIC PRINCIPLES OF CLASSICAL BALLET, Agrippina Vaganova. Great Russian theoretician, teacher explains methods for teaching classical ballet. 118 illustrations. 175pp. 5⅜ x 8½. 22036-2 Pa. $6.95

THE JUMPING FROG, Mark Twain. Revenge edition. The original story of The Celebrated Jumping Frog of Calaveras County, a hapless French translation, and Twain's hilarious "retranslation" from the French. 12 illustrations. 66pp. 5⅜ x 8½. 22686-7 Pa. $4.95

BEST REMEMBERED POEMS, Martin Gardner (ed.). The 126 poems in this superb collection of 19th- and 20th-century British and American verse range from Shelley's "To a Skylark" to the impassioned "Renascence" of Edna St. Vincent Millay and to Edward Lear's whimsical "The Owl and the Pussycat." 224pp. 5⅜ x 8½. 27165-X Pa. $5.95

COMPLETE SONNETS, William Shakespeare. Over 150 exquisite poems deal with love, friendship, the tyranny of time, beauty's evanescence, death and other themes in language of remarkable power, precision and beauty. Glossary of archaic terms. 80pp. 5$\frac{3}{16}$ x 8¼. 26686-9 Pa. $1.00

THE BATTLES THAT CHANGED HISTORY, Fletcher Pratt. Eminent historian profiles 16 crucial conflicts, ancient to modern, that changed the course of civilization. 352pp. 5⅜ x 8½. 41129-X Pa. $9.95

THE INFLUENCE OF SEA POWER UPON HISTORY, 1660–1783, A. T. Mahan. Influential classic of naval history and tactics still used as text in war colleges. First paperback edition. 4 maps. 24 battle plans. 640pp. 5⅜ x 8½. 25509-3 Pa. $14.95

THE STORY OF THE TITANIC AS TOLD BY ITS SURVIVORS, Jack Winocour (ed.). What it was really like. Panic, despair, shocking inefficiency, and a little heroism. More thrilling than any fictional account. 26 illustrations. 320pp. 5⅜ x 8½. 20610-6 Pa. $8.95

FAIRY AND FOLK TALES OF THE IRISH PEASANTRY, William Butler Yeats (ed.). Treasury of 64 tales from the twilight world of Celtic myth and legend: "The Soul Cages," "The Kildare Pooka," "King O'Toole and his Goose," many more. Introduction and Notes by W. B. Yeats. 352pp. 5⅜ x 8½. 26941-8 Pa. $8.95

BUDDHIST MAHAYANA TEXTS, E. B. Cowell and others (eds.). Superb, accurate translations of basic documents in Mahayana Buddhism, highly important in history of religions. The Buddha-karita of Asvaghosha, Larger Sukhavativyuha, more. 448pp. 5⅜ x 8½. 25552-2 Pa. $12.95

ONE TWO THREE . . . INFINITY: Facts and Speculations of Science, George Gamow. Great physicist's fascinating, readable overview of contemporary science: number theory, relativity, fourth dimension, entropy, genes, atomic structure, much more. 128 illustrations. Index. 352pp. 5⅜ x 8½. 25664-2 Pa. $9.95

EXPERIMENTATION AND MEASUREMENT, W. J. Youden. Introductory manual explains laws of measurement in simple terms and offers tips for achieving accuracy and minimizing errors. Mathematics of measurement, use of instruments, experimenting with machines. 1994 edition. Foreword. Preface. Introduction. Epilogue. Selected Readings. Glossary. Index. Tables and figures. 128pp. 5³/₈ x 8¹/₂. 40451-X Pa. $6.95

DALÍ ON MODERN ART: The Cuckolds of Antiquated Modern Art, Salvador Dalí. Influential painter skewers modern art and its practitioners. Outrageous evaluations of Picasso, Cézanne, Turner, more. 15 renderings of paintings discussed. 44 calligraphic decorations by Dalí. 96pp. 5⅜ x 8½. (Available in U.S. only.) 29220-7 Pa. $5.95

ANTIQUE PLAYING CARDS: A Pictorial History, Henry René D'Allemagne. Over 900 elaborate, decorative images from rare playing cards (14th–20th centuries): Bacchus, death, dancing dogs, hunting scenes, royal coats of arms, players cheating, much more. 96pp. 9¼ x 12¼. 29265-7 Pa. $12.95

MAKING FURNITURE MASTERPIECES: 30 Projects with Measured Drawings, Franklin H. Gottshall. Step-by-step instructions, illustrations for constructing handsome, useful pieces, among them a Sheraton desk, Chippendale chair, Spanish desk, Queen Anne table and a William and Mary dressing mirror. 224pp. 8⅛ x 11¼. 29338-6 Pa. $16.95

THE FOSSIL BOOK: A Record of Prehistoric Life, Patricia V. Rich et al. Profusely illustrated definitive guide covers everything from single-celled organisms and dinosaurs to birds and mammals and the interplay between climate and man. Over 1,500 illustrations. 760pp. 7½ x 10⅛. 29371-8 Pa. $29.95

Prices subject to change without notice.